Social Responsiveness of Infants

DISCARDED

Summary Publications* in the Johnson & Johnson Baby
Products Company Pediatric Round Table series:

*Maternal Attachment and Mothering Disorders:
A Round Table*
Edited by Marshall H. Klaus, M.D.,
Treville Leger and
Mary Anne Trause, Ph.D.

The Social Responsiveness of Infants
Edited by Evelyn B. Thoman, Ph.D.
and Sharland Trotter

Play and Learning
Edited by Paul Chance, Ph.D.
and Brian Sutton-Smith, Ph.D.

*See Bibliography for listing of counterpart scientific publications.

Social Responsiveness of Infants

A Round Table:
Edited by Evelyn B. Thoman, Ph.D.
and Sharland Trotter

Sponsored by
Johnson & Johnson
BABY PRODUCTS COMPANY

Library of Congress Catologing in Publication Data
Main entry under title:

The Social responsiveness of infants.

(Johnson & Johnson Baby Products Company
pediatric round table series; 2)
Bibliography: p.
Includes index.
1. Infant psychology—Addresses, essays, lectures. 2. Mother and child—Addresses, essays,
lectures. 3. Child psychology—Research—Addresses,
essays, lectures. I. Thoman, Evelyn B.
II. Trotter, Sharland. III. Johnson & Johnson,
inc. Baby Products Company. IV. Series: Johnson
and Johnson, inc. Baby Products Company. Johnson
& Johnson Baby Products Company pediatric round
table series; 2.
BF723.I6S56   155.4'22   78-14247
ISBN 0-931562-01-5
Copyright © 1978 by Johnson & Johnson Baby Products Company

This book is dedicated to the parents and children who participated in these studies and thereby provided a legacy of understanding and information for parents and children in the future.

Contents

Section III Ontogeny of the Mother-Infant Relationship

Participants

Kathryn Barnard, RN, Ph.D.
Professor of Nursing
University of Washington
Seattle, Washington

Greta N. Basil
Creative Supervisor
Young & Rubicam International, Inc.
New York, New York

Matthew H. Basile
Creative Supervisor
Young & Rubicam International, Inc.
New York, New York

Mr. William H. Bortree
Group Product Director
Johnson & Johnson
Baby Products Company
New Brunswick, New Jersey

T. G. R. Bower, Ph.D.
Lecturer
Department of Psychology
University of Edinburgh
Edinburgh, Scotland

Richard A. Chase, M.D.
President
Environmental Programs, Inc.
Baltimore, Maryland

Victor H. Denenberg, Ph.D.
Professor
Department of Biobehavioral Sciences
The University of Connecticut
Storrs, Connecticut

Rita B. Eisenberg, Ph.D.
Director, Bioacoustic Laboratory
Research Institute
St. Joseph Hospital
Lancaster, Pennsylvania

Gavin Hildick-Smith, M.D.
Director of Medical Affairs
Johnson & Johnson
New Brunswick, New Jersey

John H. Kennel, M.D.
Professor of Pediatrics
Department of Pediatrics
Case Western Reserve University
Cleveland, Ohio

Anneliese Korner, Ph.D.
Adjunct Professor of Psychiatry
Stanford University School of Medicine
Stanford, California

Lewis P. Lipsitt, Ph.D.
Professor of Psychology and
    Medical Science
Brown University
Providence, Rhode Island

William Mason, Ph.D.
Professor of Psychology
Department of Psychology
University of California,
Davis, California

Hanuš Papoušek, M.D.
Professor
Max-Planck Institute for Psychiatry
University of Munich
Munich, West Germany

Arthur H. Parmelee, M.D.
Professor of Pediatrics
Head of Division of Child
    Development, U.C.L.A.
Los Angeles, California

Harriet L. Rheingold, Ph.D.
Research Professor
Department of Psychology
University of North Carolina
Chapel Hill, North Carolina

Mr. Robert B. Rock, Jr.
Director of Professional Relations
Johnson & Johnson
Baby Products Company
New Brunswick, New Jersey

Louis W. Sander, M.D.
Department of Psychiatry
University of Colorado
    Medical Center
Denver, Colorado

Steven Sawchuk, M.D.
Director of Medical Services
Johnson & Johnson
Baby Products Company
New Brunswick, New Jersey

Bruck Semple, M.D.
Director of Medical
    and Regulatory Affairs
Johnson & Johnson
Baby Products Company
New Brunswick, New Jersey

Daniel N. Stern, M.D.
Payne Whitney Clinic
New York Hospital-Cornell
University Medical Center
525 East 68th Street
New York, New York

Evelyn B. Thoman, Ph.D.
Associate Professor
Department of Biobehavioral Sciences
The University of Connecticut
Storrs, Connecticut

John S. Watson, Ph.D.
Associate Professor of Psychology
Department of Psychology
University of California
Berkeley, California

Leon Yarrow, Ph.D.
Chief, Social and Behavioral Sciences
    Branch
N.I.C.H.D.
National Institutes of Health
Bethesda, Maryland

Preface

This publication summarizes the second in the series of Pediatric Round Tables sponsored by the Johnson & Johnson Baby Products Company. In undertaking sponsorship of the series, the company has sought to develop for child health-care specialists and parents information at the leading edge of new concepts in child development.

The Round Table on "The Origins of the Infant's Social Responsiveness" consisted of three segments: 1) The Infants Rhythms and Responses as Preparation for Partnership, 2) Developing Designs for Viewing the Infant as a Social Being, 3) Ontogeny of the Mother-Infant Relationship. The material covered provides insights into the infant's sensitivities for responses to his new world and his developing capabilities during the first year of life—with primary concern for the infant's role as a member of the mother-infant system. As this volume reflects the pooled knowledge of a major group of internationally recognized scientists, it is offered by the Johnson & Johnson Baby Products Company as a contribution to the knowledge and literature in the field of child development.

R. B. Rock, Jr.
Director of Professional Relations

Foreword

By T. Berry Brazelton, M.D.
Associate Professor of Pediatrics
Harvard Medical School and
Chief, Child Development Unit
Children's Hospital Medical Center
Boston, Massachusetts

In the phylogenetic scale, the human infant has the longest and most dependent relationship with his caregivers. Since it is difficult to believe that nature has not been purposeful in its adaptation over the centuries, one wonders what the adaptive purpose of such a prolonged period must be. Complexity of cognitive and social function seem to represent a major goal for human development. In a world as demanding as ours, a set of oversimplified responses is not adaptive. The capacity to make rapid decisions, to adapt to completely novel and unexpected events, to respond to emotional stresses and disruptions without being overwhelmed, to be able to love and be loved, to nurture as well as find nurturance in a too often unloving society—all of these could be seen as goals that require this long period of dependency in infancy. Parents as cultural representatives must adapt these goals and cultural expectations to the infant's capacity to learn the necessary skills for survival and a rewarding future. This is an increasingly large order for new, inexperienced young parents. And in our lonely nuclear society there are far too few signposts to help them understand their job. It is no wonder that they turn to advice-giving books on child-rearing for the answers that

might have come from experience in childhood in a culture where children participated in the rearing of siblings or cousins, or from a nurturing, extended family where grandparents, aunts, and uncles were on hand to support and pass on generations of experience in child-rearing. But our young nuclear families have none of these guidelines. Far too few parents have anyone to turn to for guidelines, for approval, or for the nurturing in a period of stress which in turn fuels a parent's capacity to nurture. Most young parents must find the way alone. I do not believe that advice, written or visually presented, offers more than a superficial kind of backup for the decision-making necessary to parenting. I do feel that understanding oneself and one's baby is the basis for the feeling of competence necessary for enjoying one's child and being successful as a parent. In turn, this feeling of competence is transmitted from parent to child, and is the base of a child's self-esteem. Hence, my goal for young parents is that they have opportunities for understanding themselves and their babies as they develop together.

This volume includes the research insights from some of the most elegant infant researchers in the world today. An understanding of the complexity of the infant, which is the basis for his adaptation to his new world, can offer new parents the opportunity to understand him and their reactions to him. Hence, these papers can be of real value to parents and to professionals who are concerned with the problems of parenting.

The "new" research that presents the marvelous complexity of infants, and sets his capacity to make decisions about what he will not attend to in his environment, is exemplified by the research of Drs. Eisenberg and Lipsitt. It becomes evident that he is not at the mercy of an environment that is not entirely appropriate for him. He can shut out noises (such as those of a delivery room or noisy newborn nursery) and can choose to respond with all of his attention to his mother's soft voice. He can learn quickly from brief, but appropriate, experiences because he is born with programmed choices for certain sounds and tastes. Eisenberg's insights into the levels of central nervous system function that play into complex auditory processing offer clinicians a diagnostic base for assessing the integrity of the brain at birth. Her observations of the richness of the neonate's responses are coupled with her understanding of the location of his musical or intonational capacities in the right side of his brain, and speech in the left side. These offer professionals and parents the opportunity to make their own observations of neonatal responses and to understand the neurological bases for them. How rewarding for parents and professionals who value the opportunity to observe and understand the newborn baby's complexity! Lipsitt's documentation of the infant's capacity to differentiate

so carefully among tastes maps the marvelous decision-making capacities in this area, which are present in the newborn.

The animal researchers, Drs. Mason and Dennenberg, invite us to reconsider the kind of environments we provide for our babies. Are we content with environments full of inanimate objects but devoid of opportunities for learning about oneself that are presented by caring and interacting persons? Mason's work with monkeys, which separates the variables necessary to the development of curiosity, social skills, and an active rather than a passive relationship with one's environment, should be a warning to all of us who are concerned with providing appropriate environments for infants, such as hospital nurseries, day care centers, or other substitutes for the richly rewarding relationships of an attached, attentive mother and father.

Drs. Korner and Parmelee point to some of the opportunities for enriching the environments for premature and stressed infants, and warn us of the dangers of overloading such infants' already stressed neurological systems by inappropriate or too much stimulation. Their research also points out the importance of reconsidering positive sensory experiences as organizational opportunities for nervous systems that may be at risk for ultimate integrity. Perhaps we could not only speed up the recovery of stressed babies but also improve their outcome. As nurse-researcher Barnard points out, if we can present the anxious parents of a premature infant with a better organized and responsive baby at the time of his discharge, we will have improved his and their opportunities for attachment to each other. This research presents nursing and pediatric professionals with the challenge of rethinking the ways our hospital nurseries and premature-infant facilities operate; particularly, it offers the opportunity for improving the future outcome of high-risk infants by allowing for more sensitive attention to the baby's recovery and organization. As Dr. Kennell points out, attention to his mother's recovery can be critical to her capacity to nurture him and provide him with a rich future.

Most exciting to me in this volume is the collection of essays concerned with the infant's social organization and his learning to master his environment. Bower's chapter on how he proceeds from abstract, general concepts to specific ones is a real opportunity to understand the spurts and regressions that make up all of a child's developmental progress. For example, Bower places awareness of strangers more clearly in the context of learning about attachment, and those for whom the child cares, than anxiety about strangeness. I have always felt that the peaks of reactions to strangers in infancy were really peaks of intense curiosity, and that they accompanied spurts of learning about new areas of his world.

Watson's elegant essay on understanding the limits of contingency and non-contingency makes marvelous sense in an environment that must always be a mixture. His insights into how the infant learns from both flexibly contingent and structured events again points to the infant's marvelously rich adaptiveness, as it does to the value of a richly complex environment for the infant.

Drs. Hanuš and Mechthild Papoušek have been pioneers in helping us to understand the adaptive learning processes of small infants. They point to the forces in the infant that are fueled by social opportunities for play with caregivers. Drs. Yarrow and Thoman reinforce the primary opportunities for learning about himself and his environment which parents and caregivers offer to developing infants. Sander and Stern begin to establish the temporal bases for interaction on which all learning is built. Their elegantly detailed studies have begun to help us understand the underlying regulatory systems being shaped by the environment, and give us an opportunity to see the rhythms and "games" present in a normal environment as fuel for the infant's learning about himself and the self-regulation needed to succeed in his world. By the same token, a better understanding of the these basic regulatory processes in normal infants gives us the opportunity to identify and understand the dysrhythmias and asynchrony that underlie the regulatory systems in a damaged or at-risk infant. By understanding the violation of these basic rhythms in such an infant, perhaps we can help parents who must adapt to and make it with him. For a violation of these rhythms is an assault on their unconscious expectations for him, which is coupled with their conscious grief over his not being the perfect infant they might have visualized.

This is a rich volume of exciting work in the processes of infancy and early development. It offers parents a sophisticated opportunity to understand the babies with whom they are living and working. It offers clinicians and professionals new and valuable insights into normal development. The value of applying these insights to abnormal or deviant development is great. The opportunity for using these theoretical approaches to enhance hospital and other substitute environments for enriching the potential development of the infant's central nervous system and psychophysiological organization is a real challenge to all of us in the field of pediatrics and pediatric nursing.

Introduction

By Evelyn B. Thoman and Sharland Trotter

Infancy is a fascinating and critical period of human development. Until fairly recently, however, it was like an unexplored continent; very few techniques existed for discovering what goes on in the mind of a baby. It was widely assumed, therefore, that the infant, especially in the neonatal period, is a passive and incomplete organism who slowly becomes, through a series of linear developmental progressions, a complete organism: a child, then an adult.

Over the last decade there has been a remarkable growth in the scientific techniques available for investigating infancy. The result has been an explosion of information about all facets of development during infancy. Like the college sophomore and the laboratory rat, the human infant has become a favorite laboratory subject, and the rapidly accumulating evidence documents quite clearly that the young infant, far from being a *tabula rasa,* is even at birth endowed with an impressive array of capabilities.

Such findings are relatively new, however, and many people do not fully appreciate their implications. It is therefore particularly fitting that the Johnson & Johnson Baby Products Company should sponsor a conference devoted to exploring some of these early capacities, with a primary emphasis on the infant as a socially responsive being.

The conference participants—whose current work is summarized in the pages that follow—represent some of the foremost researchers in the field of early infancy. Their contributions span many diverse areas of investigation, ranging from the most rigorous laboratory studies to naturalistic observations in the home; and from highly focused studies of such processes as perception, learning and motivation to more broadly focused research on social behavior. The conference provided them with an opportunity to exchange ideas and findings; to present film and video-tapes as well as substantive research reports; in short, to learn from one another about new methods and techniques, and to formulate new questions about what that mysterious creature—the newborn baby—is like from the time of birth.

The conference papers and discussions, although representing sharply divergent views in some areas, together reflect a changing view of the infant as a being exquisitely well-prepared to interact with his environment, and particularly with the people in it. The participants considered seriously several issues: the possibility that infants have a rich affective life from their earliest days; that even normal infants vary widely in their sensitivities, response capabilities, motor behaviors, and other characteristics; and that an evolutionary perspective may be useful in exploring the newborn infant's biological preparation for effective interaction with the environment.

For example, the Czech pediatrician and psychologist, Papoušek, addresses himself explicitly to the question of interrelations between biological and social factors in the infant's behavioral organization from the time of birth. Other participants affirm the infant's impressive organization and coordinating capabilities, which are apparent in the variety of patterned events to which the newborn is responsive: patterns of sounds, particularly those present in human speech (Eisenberg); patterns of visual stimuli (Bower and Watson); the temporal patterning of events (Sander, Stern, Lipsitt, and Watson); and patterns of social stimuli (Mason, Sander, Stern, and Papoušek). That an absence of patterned stimuli may have detrimental effects is suggested by Korner, whose work has sought to provide compensatory movement stimulation for premature babies. Additional complex characteristics of very young infants include behaviors that reflect cognitive processes involving hypothesis making and testing (Bower, Papoušek, Stern, and Watson).

The infant's competence as perceiver, performer and problem solver has been richly documented, both here and elsewhere. But the complexity of an individual infant is far more than the total sum of all the identifiable competencies, impressive though they may be. A major theme that emerges from the observations and analyses reported in the following pages is that the infant cannot be properly understood outside the context of his ongoing interactions with his mother (or other principal caretaker). And interactions, even the very earliest ones, are two-way affairs. Denenberg makes an eloquent plea for studying developmental processes from a systems point of view that can take such interactions into account.

Indeed, the mother–infant relationship has come increasingly to be viewed as a system in which both partners are engaged in a continuing process of mutual modification. This is compellingly clear in the work of Thoman, who shows how difficult it is to conceive of either partner as "causing" the behavior of the other. Instead, interaction is seen as a process with an accumulation of its own history.

A concern with process is another related theme that appears again and again. Interactions are never static; process, by definition, occurs in time. In order to understand the infant's organization, it is therefore necessary to observe and describe the numerous changes that occur within the earliest period of life. This will yield in turn an understanding of the developmental processes by which the infant modifies and is modified by the environment. Sander's work in particular shows that from the beginning an infant's behavior is organized in time, and the evident periodicity, which is at first internally regulated, very soon after birth becomes linked to external events, particularly to caretaker activities. Sander points out that the tasks of adaptation demanded of the infant include the development of synchrony with the mother's temporal rhythms of caretaking and interaction.

The temporal patterning of mother–infant interactions is further elaborated by Stern, who demonstrates the extent to which the mother will exaggerate, slow down, and repeat both her verbal and nonverbal behavior in order to maintain or heighten the infant's interest and attention. Mothers also (as pointed out by several of the participants) spend a lot of time watching intently for cues from the infant, so that they can gauge the timing and appropriateness of their interventions. Thus, each mother–infant pair develops its own particular style of interaction, with rhythms and routines that are unique to that mother and that baby—a phenomenon that Bower suggests may play a significant role in the infant's development of the classic attachment behaviors and separation anxiety.

The emphasis on mother–infant interaction has clearly given a new direction to the study of early social behavior. As a result, new questions are being asked and new methods and techniques are being used to answer them. The intensive study of minute sequences of behavior, made possible through the development of film and videotape techniques, among other things, also raises a host of methodological issues. For example, an observation session lasting only a few minutes can generate a tremendous amount of data, which is then analyzed in terms of fractions of a second. Not surprisingly, therefore, samples tend to be quite small, which makes the problem of generalizing findings a serious one. Moreover, the presence of obtrusive equipment and/or personnel, whether in the home or in a laboratory setting, tends to exacerbate the issue. Yarrow and Anderson describe the rather disorderly data base from which inferences about parent–infant interactions are drawn, and both Denenberg and Rheingold point to the need for replications.

Meanwhile, as developmental scientists struggle to make their methodologies match their conceptual models, clinicians are also proposing new interactional approaches in the area of assessment and prediction. Parmelee's notion of a "cumulative risk score" involves a broad spectrum of social and physiological variables that are assessed at successive ages to identify patterns of deviance at each age and patterns of change over time. His approach reflects a realistic recognition that the infant–environment system may serve either to aggravate or ameliorate developmental handicaps. Similarly, Barnard has explored successive interactional assessment procedures for diagnostic purposes, and Klaus and Kennell have carried out numerous interactional studies aimed at exploring the problems that may stem from the infants being separated from their mothers in the period immediately after birth.

In sum, new perspectives in the field of early infancy reflect changing assumptions about the nature of the infant and about the nature of research in this area. Like Renaissance artists, scientists and clinicians alike are relinquishing the myth of the infant as a miniature adult—thought to be helpless, passive, and unfeeling—in favor of the view that infancy is a different state from maturity; it is not necessarily a matter of moving from the simple to the complex, from the unfinished infant to the unfinished adult. The

participants at this conference are in
agreement that the stage of infancy is
important in and of itself. The
remarkable capabilities of the
newborn infant that have been
already "discovered" are only an
introduction to what may be expected
as the world of the infant is explored
in its own right.

Rita B. Eisenberg, Ph.D.

Stimulus Significance as a Determinant of Infant
Responses to Sound

Rita Eisenberg, Director of the Bioacoustic Laboratory in Lancaster, Pennsylvania, has for many years been concerned with problems of language and hearing. The focus of her research is on newborn life, and a large part of her effort is directed at building a model that , as she puts it, "relates what comes into the ears and what goes out of the mouth."

In Eisenberg's view, auditory adaptations in man have to do primarily with the organization of verbal information, although they also bear importantly upon such nonverbal functions as the development of social responsiveness. She observes that "mothers probably have soothed their babies by humming or singing to them since time immemorial. Many, if not all, adults have nonverbal vocabulary of cooing and clucking nonsense sounds that they trot out, consciously or unconsciously, only for communication with the very young." And all of us, she says, "respond on an emotional level to environmental sounds and to nuances of voice that color and sometimes even contradict the verbal contents of speech."

For Eisenberg, the realities of human hearing are, first, that hearing and listening are not the same thing, since as we all know from experience, it is perfectly possible to hear without listening. Secondly, in man, as in lower species, there is a systematic relationship between what goes into the ears and what comes out of the mouth; that is, the sounds processed by our auditory mechanisms and produced by our vocal mechanisims are physically matched. Finally, it is clear that people automatically sort out enviromental and speech sounds, process them differentially, and respond to them, on a number of levels. In other words, says Eisenberg, "we somehow hear different things in different ways at the same time." What all this adds up to is that "hearing is a hierarchy of auditory functions that presumably must be served by a hierarchy of special purpose mechanisms."

There are five basic questions that underlie Dr. Eisenberg's efforts to establish a testable model of the auditory system: What properties of the central nervous system permit us to hear different things in different ways at the same time? What mechanisms underlie our extra- ordinary auditory competence? What sensory specializations underlie our use of verbal codes? Are these mechanisms and specializations uniquely human? Are they present at birth or acquired during the course of development?

To begin with, it is by now abundantly clear that the human newborn, in comparison with other species, has an exceedingly well developed auditory system, and can respond to significant sounds from the environment. A normal baby, says Eisenberg, "emerges from the womb rather neatly equipped to organize his auditory world." Eisenberg's aim has been to determine the specific auditory processing abilities of the human infant by systematically studying infant responses to different auditory signals.

In her first studies, only overt behavioral responses were measured. Infants were observed during auditory stimulation for signs of alerting, orienting, motor activity, and reflexive responses. In subsequent studies, Eisenberg added data from electrophysiological measures. She now believes that heart rate measurement and electroencephalographic (EEG) responses from the brain surface are especially valuable for the study of infant audition. The results of the measures are correlated with the infant's "state" at the time, which varies from sound sleep to alert wakefulness.

The auditory signals that have been presented to infants include pure tones and noises that are created mechanically. These sounds are considered "constant" because their physical properties do not vary over time. Because constant signals are technically easy to produce and control, they are used extensively for auditory testing in clinics and laboratories. However, because they are not "natural" sounds, it is believed they may be less biologically meaningful to humans. Nevertheless, because of their technical simplicity,

Eisenberg and others have used constant signals to test infants' responses to such acoustic parameters as frequency (pitch) and sound pressure level (loudness).

Eisenberg has also studied infants' responses to multidimensional sounds, such as tonal sequences and sounds that occur in spoken language. She classifies these sounds as "patterned" because their physical components are invariant only in relation to each other. Presenting patterned signals in either a laboratory or clinical setting poses a number of technical problems, but they more nearly approximate sounds in the natural environment.

Eisenberg and others have found that infants respond very much as adults do to such acoustic features of constant signals as frequency and intensity. Low frequencies, for example, which tend to have a soothing effect on infants, also typically evoke gross motor activity. High frequencies, on the other hand, tend to cause distress rather than inhibit it, and elicit body stilling, or "fixation" responses. Behavioral responses to low frequencies are best elicited during dozing or light sleep, whereas responses to high frequencies are more easily evoked during wakeful states.

It is felt that these differential infant responses correspond later in life to the emotional reactions that adults have to different sound frequencies. Indeed, Eisenberg says, "they are reflected in the electrophysiological responses of adult subjects, in the acoustic properties of our musical instruments and alarm signals, in the kinds of sound we find annoying, in the words we use to describe our reactions, and perhaps even in the ways we store acoustic information." In sum, whatever the context in which psychological responses to sound are studied, low frequencies invariably seem to have "good" or "pleasure" connotations, and high frequencies the reverse.

According to Eisenberg, these findings have important implications for our thinking about developmental processes in hearing. First, they suggest that differential "tuning" to the frequencies of language may be built in during intrauterine life. Second, they suggest that the newborn's unique response to high-frequency signals may be as much a phylogenetic relic as the Moro reflex. And finally, they suggest that qualitative judgments of sound in adult life, such as "noisiness," "pleasantness," and the like, may have their roots in preadapted mechanisms referable to phylogenetic history.

Responses to sound pressure level, or intensity, also follow similar patterns throughout the life cycle. As with adults, infant brain wave potentials tend to increase in size as sounds become louder, and to be "larger" as the auditory stimulus becomes more intense; also, behavioral responses become increasingly agitated as sound intensity increases. Such responses lead Eisenberg to believe that the neuronal mechanisms for processing intensity may be fully operational at birth. She further speculates that "loudness and other so-called 'natural' dimensions of sound may have their roots in preadapted mechanisms referable to species history."

These findings about infant responses to pitch and loudness have been derived almost exclusively from studies with "constant" signals, such as pure tones and band noises, which differ importantly from multidimensional or "patterned" signals in the effects they have on infant behavior. The most outstanding effect of constant signals, according to Eisenberg, is nonspecificity. She explains that it is generally difficult for observers to tell when an infant is responding to a stimulus like a pure tone, because the behavior differs so little from nonstimulus behavior. Vocal responses can almost never be elicited by constant signals, and, says Eisenberg, "the most sophisticated visual reaction found is a kind of wide-eyed 'what-is-it?' look usually considered to be orienting behavior."

In contrast, infant responses to patterned stimuli are highly specific. When patterns of ascending and descending tones or synthetically produced speech sounds are presented, even naive observers can reliably detect changes in infant behavior. Infants may show signs of arousal, may suddenly cry or stop crying, their pupils may dilate, and sometimes they will turn their heads, presumably toward the sound source. Heart rate and brain wave changes continue as patterned stimuli are repeated, whereas repetitions of constant stimuli do not produce heart rate or EEG changes. Infant brain waves also show longer latencies to patterned then to unpatterned (constant) stimuli. These differences in response indicate a perceptually mature auditory system in the infant, and they also suggest that the infant's selective responses to tonal patterns and speech sounds reflect a high level of neuronal organization. The kinds of differences found in infant response patterns also imply that natural, patterned stimuli may be more useful than constant signals for the further study of infants' auditory processing abilities.

Eisenberg infers from her own and other studies that changes in auditory behavior—including vocalizations— reflect "preprogrammed" alterations in neuronal organization that are triggered by appropriate environmental demands. She speculates that auditory specializations prerequisite to language perception are present in the newborn period, and she further proposes that the auditory system is organized and develops in a hierarchical fashion. What this implies, says Eisenberg, is that "human beings, as the most complex of creatures and the only ones to communicate by verbal codes, will have a variety of low-level auditory coding mechanisms that they share with other species, as well as certain uniquely specialized higher level mechanisms for coding speech sounds."

Eisenberg describes a hierarchical model with four levels of processing, each level being a derivative of the level below. The lowest level in the hierarchy essentially filters out low from high-frequency auditory information. High frequencies are channeled out at the first level for brain stem storage and/or processing, while low frequencies are transmitted for specific coding to higher levels of the nervous system. This circuit, present at birth as a phylogenetic relic of approach-withdrawal behavior, is elaborated into an organized "affective" or emotional system during the course of development. This lowest level possibly involves the old brain, particularly the limbic system.

At the second level, incoming signals are refined and extracted for further processing or storage at this level. Eisenberg believes that operations at this level bear at least indirectly upon language acquisition. She suggests that a grading mechanism operates for loudness perception, and a tuning mechanism for frequency analysis. A differential mechanism for responding to intensity of sounds would allow the developing infant to orient to significant language sounds. Selective tuning to the critical frequencies of speech might lead not only to preferential orientation towards spoken language, but also to preparing the child's speech apparatus for articulatory movements later in development.

The third and fourth levels are more speculative because substantive information on neonatal response is available for only a few patterned stimuli. However, what is known about perceptual processing suggests that functional asymmetries may exist during early life. Thus, the third level may process patterned stimuli that have intonational or musical characteristics, but not the special time characteristics of speech. Such nonspeech sounds presumably could be processed by the nondominant, usually right, hemisphere of the brain. The fourth and highest level of auditory processing, which occurs in the dominant, usually left, hemisphere, is thought to involve the reception and processing of speech information.

One valuable prediction that could be derived from this admittedly tentative model is that damage to the central auditory system would affect its function differentially, depending upon the level at which pathology occurred. Eisenberg believes that the hierarchical levels develop sequentially, so that neuronal damage at a given stage of development should be reflected in a specific pattern of difficulty.

Eisenberg states that this model should be useful in providing testable predictions about brain development in infancy and corresponding auditory abilities. She sees her model as a means for studying the auditory system and gaining a better understanding of auditory development in infancy. One result of such understanding could be the diagnosis and treatment of language disabilities in children earlier than is now possible.

Finally, Eisenberg speculates on the implications of her model for the development of social responsiveness in infancy. What her model says, in effect, is that the infant normally is predisposed to respond to certain kinds of sensory stimuli that are not only pleasurable, but embodied in the person of the caregiver, usually the mother. "She is the most ubiquitous object in his environment," says Eisenberg, "and, as such, an amalgam of prepotent stimuli to which the infant, by virtue of his neuronal organization, is programmed to respond. Her voice, which constitutes a patterned stimulus, is the most important sound he hears because it is presented, under wakeful conditions and at close quarters, during feeding and other care-giving activities. Her face, which also can be considered a patterned stimulus, is the object of closest regard during these activities. Further, these auditory and visual stimuli are associated not only with other percepts, but also with physical satisfactions; that is, with tactile and taste and olfactory sensations aroused during satiation of hunger, cessation of discomfort, and so on."

Eisenberg feels, moreover, that given a normal infant and an adequate caregiver, "these sensory perceptions of the infant constitute the roots of both social and intellectual development."

John S. Watson, Ph. D.

Perception of Contingency as a Determinant of Social Responsiveness

Those doing research on social behavior have typically studied the power of different stimulus objects to induce a response from social animals, including species from rats to human infants. There are basically two schools of thought on the origins of social responsiveness in humans. According to *empiricist,* or social learning theory, people "learn" response patterns from specific encounters with the natural environment. For example, by the time they are six weeks old, nearly all babies have begun to smile most engagingly at human faces. Empiricists would claim that babies smile because they have learned to associate faces with pleasurable stimulation, or with relief from the discomfort of being cold, wet, hungry, or thirsty. The *nativist* argument, on the other hand, holds that social objects are "recognized" innately and that responsiveness develops in a biologically predetermined manner. Nativists claim that smiling is an innate response that is genetically predetermined to appear at a predictable time. To bolster their case, they point to evidence that all babies begin to smile on a remarkably similar schedule—at the conceptual age of forty-six weeks—regardless of how much time they've had to experience adult care, or to associate faces with pleasure or relief from pain. That is, premature babies don't

smile any earlier; post-term babies don't smile any later.

The nativist and empiricist perspectives are in absolute opposition regarding the necessity of prior experience in determining social responsiveness. Notably, however, both schools of thought have emphasized research on the purely physical properties of stimuli. For instance, various arrangements of facial features (upside down, scrambled, regular) have been shown to produce varied responses from human infants at different ages.

In contrast, psychologist John S. Watson, at the University of California at Berkeley, is interested in the relationship between a baby's behavior and the consequences of that baby's active interaction with the world. The traditional focus on the physical, says Watson, limits our view of what constitutes experience. He believes that learning about cause and effect and discovering that one's own actions can influence events provide the basis for social responsiveness in the human infant. According to Watson, the mechanism by which social learning occurs involves the infant's perception of a contingent relationship between some particular behavior and an event in the external world, and not through repeated associations with the physical features of objects.

When a newborn cries, for

example, the mother will usually offer breast or bottle, and usually the infant will suck. Later in infancy, additional responses by the mother will follow her baby's cries, such as changing diapers, holding, or soothing. Mothers learn to differentiate between infant cries produced by hunger and those due to other causes. Thus, certain regular causes and effects, or "contingencies," are established between the infant's crying and the mother's caregiving.

In play situations, adults are most likely to engage infants in what are basically contingency-detection games. For example, an adult may sit opposite a baby and every time the baby turns around the adult will proffer a toy, or tickle the baby's tummy, or make a face. All such games present the baby with an opportunity to detect a contingency between some specific behavior and an event in the world outside.

Watson believes that social responses develop through just such perceptions of cause and effect relationships. He proposes that the infant learns to recognize and respond to social objects (things, as well as people) by discovering what to do to make a particular event happen. To explore this hypothesis, Watson created a situation in which eight-week-old infants could control the movements of mobiles placed over their cribs by moving their heads a certain way on special pressure-sensitive pillows. After several days of only ten minutes of such experience, mothers reported that infants smiled and cooed exuberantly during this "play." No such responses were reported from the mothers of infants who had no control of the mobile. Evidently, physical pleasure or pain

played no role here. The infants were not being "rewarded" with milk or pleasurable handling. Thus, the babies' exuberant smiles indicate what might be termed an intellectual pleasure, the pleasure of having solved a problem and of being in control of some part of the world.

Watson has also investigated an infant's ability to perceive contingencies, by systematically varying the contingent relations between the baby's behavior and subsequent events. He has done this in two ways. The first, which has been extensively studied in laboratory animals, most notably by B. F. Skinner and his colleagues, involves varying the number of times an animal is rewarded for a given behavior. Such "reinforcement" can occur continuously—every response is rewarded—or partially—only some proportion of responses are followed by the reward, or "stimulus."

The second kind of contingency is actually a nonrelation in the sense that the stimulus (reward) occurs some number of times without regard to the behavior. Watson calls this "noncontingent stimulation." The simultaneous occurrence of reinforcement conditions and noncontingent stimulation actually represents natural relations between people and their environment better than reinforcement conditions alone, but Watson believes that his research is the first to study them systematically together in infants.

To illustrate, when an infant begins to babble or coo, parents often respond by babbling, cooing, or talking to the infant in return. Psychologically, this represents "reinforcement." Partial reinforcement occurs when an infant makes sounds and the parent only occasionally responds to them. But sometimes a parent will talk to an infant when the infant has made no sound, or may talk to another person when the infant is nearby. Watson would call this "noncontingent stimulation." Thus, reinforcement and noncontingent relations can and do occur for the same behaviors and responses under natural conditions. A comprehensive explanation of the development of social interactions between infants and their parents must take into account these and other kinds of actual contingent and noncontingent events.

Watson proposes a mathematical model to explain the perception of a contingency by infants, a model based on probabilistic functions relating contingent and noncontingent stimulation. Watson's model predicts several things about infant behavior. First of all, contingency perception should be poor when a given behavior and a related event or stimulus occur too frequently or rapidly. This prediction was confirmed in a different study of eight-week-old infants and their control over mobile rotation. The babies were exposed to mobiles in their homes for ten minutes on each of seven consecutive days. On the first day the mobile did not turn. On the six subsequent days the mobile turned for one second, contingent upon the babies moving their legs on pressure-sensitive pillows. Observers watched infants' facial expressions and noted when smiling occurred.

One group of sixteen infants (Group A) showed a significant increase in daily response rate, as well as increased frequency of smiling. Another group of eight-week-old

infants (Group B) were also observed. The pillows of the Group B babies, however, were adjusted to produce twice the mobile activity of the first group. This proved excessive. The high-rate group showed neither a significant rise in response rate nor smiling rate. "It would seem," concludes Watson, "that the higher rate of response and stimulus conjunction reduced the infants' ability to perceive the contingency."

Another study conducted by Watson assessed the model's prediction that a high rate of "noncontingent," i.e., random, stimulation would also inhibit an infant's ability to detect a contingency and thus have a negative effect on learning. This study was ingeniously designed to have contingent and noncontingent occurrences of a stimulus simultaneously available. Forty fourteen-week-old infants were presented with the same learning situation as in the previous study, except that the mobile was in a laboratory room and its turning was accompanied by a bell tone. Each baby had only one session, which involved a two-minute base period (during which the mobile was not activated), a nine-minute learning period (during which the mobile was activated both contingently and noncontingently), and a three-minute extinction period (during which the mobile was again inactive). The infants were randomly assigned to four groups that differed in terms of the rate at which the mobile was activated noncontingently by a computer (five times a minute or ten times a minute with random intervals) and in terms of the probability that a leg movement would activate the mobile. "The results," says Watson, "were curious."

The weakest rise in response was, as expected, in the group that experienced partial reinforcement and a high (ten times a minute) rate of noncontingent mobile turning. To the researchers' surprise, however, the sharpest rise in response rate was in the group that experienced partial reinforcement and a moderate amount of noncontingent stimulation (that is, the mobile was activated by the computer at a rate five times per minute). Watson hypothesized that infants are most likely to detect a contingency when the rates at which reinforcement and noncontingent stimulation occur are very similar, or "matched." When these rates are too disparate, babies seem to have trouble perceiving the relation between their behavior and the stimulus events.

A final study was designed by Watson to explore further the notion of matching. A new learning situation was developed, in which the reinforcement stimulus involved the simultaneous presentation of an array of colored lights and a musical chord of pure tones. Leg movements of fourteen-week-old infants were reinforced at different rates; various noncontingent rates of stimulus presentations were also tested. Watson found that when there was a "match" between the probability of a reinforced response and the rate of noncontingent stimulation, the infants were most apt to detect the contingency between their own behavior and the resulting lights and sounds. This suggests that when, as is most often the case, there are some events that are not under the infant's control, learning will be facilitated when the infant is only partially reinforced. It also implies that babies will try to modify their responses to "match" the pattern of external events.

Extending Watson's "matching" notion to infant vocalizations, one would predict that infants will learn to vocalize best when parents respond to them frequently, although not after each babble or coo. And, in fact, this is usually what happens, since parents do sometimes speak to an infant when the infant is quiet. In effect, babies appear to learn most eagerly when the pattern of events that they can control is not too discrepant from the events they can't control.

For Watson, one is perceiving contingencies when one is perceiving control. His model includes two other kinds of contingency experiences, although these have not been empirically tested. The first is what Watson calls "stimulus control of behavior." This is the formal opposite of the kinds of situations described above, in which the infant actually learns to exercise control over the environment. Instead, this kind of contingency embodies those situations, frequent in infancy, in which the infant experiences "being controlled," as in being carried, cleaned, diapered, etc. As Watson points out, a principal organizing influence of caretaking activity is that it involves many such instances. Some may be intrinsically pleasurable, while others may be intrinsically painful (as in cleaning and changing, which commonly elicit crying). Still others may be neutral. Yet each may contribute equally to the infant's perceptions of "being controlled." Watson speculates that this fact of early life also provides a basis for the development of social responsiveness and that the perception of being controlled plays a special role in organizing social behavior, a role that probably extends well beyond the initial period of establishing the proper identity of "social objects."

Watson also describes a third type of contingency perception, which he calls "stimulus-response synchrony," and suggests that infants may be able to detect "synchronous" relations between themselves and others. Watson views synchrony as a balance between the perception of "being in control" and the perception of "being controlled." It may have special status because it implies mutual regard and, ultimately, cooperative behavior.

Watson observes that while the sensitivity of humans to the state of mutual regard seems intuitively obvious, the role that the perception of synchrony plays in developing this sensitivity remains unclear. However, other researchers have found that human newborns move their arms and legs in precise synchrony with adult speech patterns, which suggests, at the very least, a high level of perceptual acuity on the infant's part.

Thus, the perception of synchrony, or mutual controlling, could result in the development of "social cooperation" by the infant. If further research bears out Watson's model of contingency perception, the conclusion will be inescapable that social relations develop through the perception of contingent relations, the exertion of control over them, and possibly a balance of control among individuals.

T. G. R. Bower, Ph. D.

The Infant's Discovery of Objects and Mothers

Human development is characteristically viewed as a cumulative process, behavioral changes progressing in more or less orderly fashion. "Higher" psychological functions depend on "lower" psychological functions; more complex skills are built on the acquisition of simpler skills. The differing effects of blindness on subsequent development offer a striking example of this hierarchical structure, since different effects derive in great part from whether the blindness occurs during or after infancy. A congenitally blind child may never be able to master concepts of space, such as those embodied by Euclidean geometry, whereas a child blinded after the age of two typically has little difficulty. Something that happens in the first two years of life determines whether or not spatial concepts can fully emerge ten years later, around the age of twelve.

Such developmental effects are well known, but not well understood. A standard model to explain them says that young babies acquire simple stimulus–response coordinations that are later reflected in conscious verbal concepts. Recent studies have undermined the appealing simplicity of such a model, however, with the paradoxical discovery that in some cases the advent of language appears actually to destroy an earlier ability rather than building on it.

For example, by eighteen months, most children have acquired the motor coordination for predicting weight; that is, they can anticipate whether an object to be grasped will be heavy or light and make the appropriate motor response. One study looked at what happens to that ability after the child has begun to talk, particularly after having understood (and misunderstood) questions about weight. In this study, the child was handed an object (e.g., a plasticine ball) whose weight was initially overestimated or underestimated. With practice, the accuracy of the estimate improved. If the shape of the object is changed, from a ball, say, into a long, thin sausage, a one-year-old child thinks the weight has also changed. But an eighteen-month-old, who has begun to take into account (albeit nonverbally) the relationship of width and length to weight, knows that the weight has not changed. A four-and-a-half-year-old child does as well with this experiment as an eighteen month old. However, if he is *asked* whether the transformed object weighs the same as it did before, the child will typically answer that the weight has changed—because the shape has changed—and will then proceed to act on that assumption, just as a one year old would do. The experiment indicates that an erroneous verbal response has apparently undermined an ability that has been in the child's repertoire for three years.

Similarly, between six months and two years of age, babies learn to count in primitive form, and can consistently choose the greater number of beads or candies from several possible groupings. But when the child begins to talk erroneously about number, tying words like "more" to length or density, the early counting ability is lost, to be regained only with success with the verbally posed problems.

Another, and more familiar, example is to be found in the baby's response to the appearance of multiple mothers. Before the age of six months, the sight of three or more mothers who appear simultaneously is not at all disturbing to a baby, and he will gladly interact with all of them. After six months, however, the baby's increasing understanding of object identity means that he is aware that he has one, and only one, mother, and the sight of several mothers at once is quite upsetting. Yet Piaget and others have described how a two-and-a-half-year-old child, when asked by his mother where his mother is, will point to some place where she is usually to be found and say she is there. Again, the advent of language seems to destroy an earlier, nonverbal comprehension of the uniqueness of the mother.

Such apparent paradoxes continue to plague developmental psychologists, who are concerned with establishing clear connections and progressions between behaviors occurring at different ages. T. G. R. Bower, a reader and researcher at the University of Edinburgh, has proposed an alternative model of development. Instead of progressing in a straightforward, building-block fashion, development is viewed by Bower as proceeding from abstract to specific, with the baby or young child progressively elaborating his internal descriptions of objects and events to make them more and more detailed. Bower's theory would explain the seemingly paradoxical retrogressions and re-learnings described above, for it suggests that mastery of different tasks involving the same concept is not readily transferred until the child has integrated his abstract understanding with his solution of the particular problem. Likewise, it explains the need for a seeming repetition in concept acquisition.

For example, one area that has been intensively studied is development of the object concept, which is essentially the evolving comprehension of spatial relations. Very young babies appear to identify objects in terms of either their location or their motion, not comprehending that the same object can appear in different places, or that different objects can appear in the same place. But somewhere between four and five months, babies begin to amalgamate their ideas about objects and realize that an object is a single entity that can move from place to place.

Now consider the problem posed to a baby by the sight of an object moving through a tunnel. Young babies may initially refuse to look at this kind of display. But with recognition that the object that he sees on each side of the tunnel is the same object, the baby must then figure out what is happening to the object when it is out of sight. Bower suggests that the baby makes the discovery that one object can go inside another and still exist, and that this generalized (i.e., abstract) comprehension can be transferred to other situations.

Bower and his colleagues have devised some ingenious experiments to test that assumption. For example, suppose that the baby sees a toy placed inside a cup. From his experience with the tunnel, he should know that the toy is in the cup and be able to retrieve it. Bower's studies indicate that that is precisely what happens. Babies who have had weeks of practice tracking an object as it moves through a tunnel do better on the retrieval task than babies with no tracking experience. Significantly, they do *less* well than babies who are given the retrieval task after less tracking experience. In other words, babies with a limited amount of experience in the tracking exercise did best of all. This suggests that there is an optimal degree of practice in solving specific problems appropriate to the learning of the more general, or abstract, concept. Excessive concentration on the specific task detracts from the ability to generalize. For example, commercially available reaching aids work on the assumption that a simple increase in opportunities for reaching will improve and accelerate performance. In fact, they don't. In some cases, they may actually retard reaching and grasping because the baby gets used to reaching for something in the same place all the time. He learns a very specified movement and can't adapt it to an object in a different place. That is, the baby can over-specify his behavior and then cannot adapt to different situations requiring similar but not identical responses.

According to Bower, this illustrates his proposition that short-term problem solving goes from abstract to specific. The abstract comprehension will permit smooth transfer to new situations embodying the same conceptual problem. The specific solution will not. In Bower's view, if the initial problem has been reduced to specifics, the child's development to a higher level will require a re-learning phase. This seeming repetition of development, Bower suggests, is caused by "the increasing specification of the rules governing performance in the first situation, so that transfer to a new situation is not possible. The initial conceptual discovery is stored in memory and must be retrieved before accelerated performance in the new situation is permitted."

The model of development worked out by Bower and his colleagues fits well with data gleaned from experiments concerned with short-term perceptual learning and conceptual processes. But Bower's theory, as he readily concedes, faces its greatest difficulty when one attempts to apply it to social development. The most influential theorists in this area, Bowlby, for example, argue that sociability starts off as a set of specific quasi-reflex responses.

One of the traditional battlegrounds for trying to determine the origins of social responsiveness has been the smile, which emerges around the age of six weeks, to the utter delight of parents and other recipients of it. Parents are convinced that the infant's smile is a clear social act; psychologists have typically denounced them as naive, and have tried to prove instead that it is simply a reflex response to high-contrast stimuli or a variety of other nonhuman events.

Bower and his colleagues at the University of Edinburgh have evidence that should help to vindicate parents. They presented eight to ten-week-old-babies with three sets of stimuli: a white card with three pairs of black dots on it; their mother's face; and a contingency game. All three elicited smiles from the babies, but they were completely different. The dots elicited sharp, short smiles, accompanied by turning away; the mother's face elicited longer, slower smiles, and movements toward, rather than away from, the stimulus; and the contingency game elicited "big," frequently repeated smiles that were more like laughter than the other two. Bower's findings indicate that young babies, like adults, are capable of multiple smiles, appropriate to specific situations.

Further evidence of specificity has come from studies of imitation. Right from the moment of birth, says Bower, the baby realizes he is a human being and will imitate other people. This capacity has been dramatically demonstrtated in babies less than a week old. If the baby's mother, or some other adult, sticks out her tongue at the baby, the baby will begin to stick his tongue out in response. If the adult then begins to flutter her eyelashes, the baby will flutter his eyelashes back. And if the adult starts to open and close her mouth or wave her fingers, the baby will do likewise. Of course, notes Bower, the newborn will stick out his tongue, flutter his eyelashes, open his mouth, and wave his fingers spontaneously. But he will do these things far more frequently if there is

an adult model present, and actually seems to enjoy this mutual imitation game.

Bower observes that the level of organization required by these behaviors is nothing short of astonishing. Consider: How does a baby know he has a mouth? How does he know he has a tongue? And how does he know that his mouth and tongue are like the mouth and tongue he sees before him? According to Bower, there must be an incredible degree of built-in "intersensory mapping" for the baby to be able to look at an adult sticking out her tongue and transform that visual information into such well-tuned imitative behavior.

The amount of built-in intersensory coordination implied by the newborn's ability to imitate is, says Bower, "more astonishing than anything we have seen in straightforward studies of perception. The motor control of mouth, tongue, eyes, and fingers is more precise than anything we have seen in studies of neonatal motor skills. And all these capacities are bent towards what is clearly, we think, a social purpose."

Given this level of specificity, what of Bower's theory that social responsiveness begins with something abstract? He argues that these responses, specific as they are, are subclasses of a very abstract family of responses. In his view, the baby's imitation is specific to *humans*, and he points out by way of emphasis that presentation of a line that turns into a circle will elicit more or less rapt attention from young babies, but not imitation.

Similarly, a related study found that newborn babies will move in precise synchrony with a human voice, but not with a nonhuman noise. Although this so-called interactional synchrony is clearly a quite specific behavior, it is based, as is the imitation ability on something broader. "There seems to be," says Bower, "a very abstract awareness that 'I am human' and 'they are human' and 'I am like them.'"

A more interesting case is how "I am human" gets transformed into "I am a girl" or "I am a boy." Research has shown that by the age of ten months, infants prefer to look at pictures of other infants of the same sex.

Bower thus argues that "social responsiveness is an innate human capacity. The earliest awareness is of nothing more specific than 'humanness,' a very abstract awareness that is gradually specified through categories such as gender to awareness of a specific personal identity." During infancy too, says Bower, the child acquires abstract ideas about other people (basically nice versus basically not nice). These abstract ideas about self and others generate specific rules and behaviors for coping with people.

He further argues that the classic attachment behaviors, separation anxiety and stranger fear, also fit his model. They are, he maintains, directly analogous to the repetition effects described earlier. Separation anxiety, according to Bower's theory, represents what he would call a "failure of transfer due to over-specification." He explains that the baby's inborn strategies for signaling his humanity to others—strategies like imitation and interactional synchrony—become over-specified. From the moment of birth, babies are ready to communicate with others.

Typically, they learn to communicate most frequently and effectively with their mothers. Gradually, the mother–infant pair develops its own particular style of interaction, with well worked out routines that are specific to that mother and that baby. Thus, when the mother leaves her baby wih someone else, she is leaving him with someone who doesn't speak the same language he does, and doesn't respond to the familiar social gestures the baby has come to depend upon. "The baby is effectively left alone," says Bower, "his communication partner gone. He is isolated from other adults by the very specificity and development of the communication routines he shares with his mother."

Bower's theory thus turns the standard model of development on its head. For in his model "higher" (more abstract) structures precede "lower" (more specific) structures.

What are the possible applications of Bower's theoretical work? He hopes that, "our research will lead to an understanding of normal developmental processes with all the predictive and intervention possibilities that implies. By normal, we mean sociologically, economically, and medically normal. There can be no reason for intervening or interfering with these infants in any direct way. Our responsibilities must surely lie with the abnormal child. In those cases we know how they will deviate from normal, and we have a good ethical reason for trying to normalize abnormal. It is only by asking why abnormal *is* abnormal that we can define abnormality better.

"Most of the 1,000 or so mothers we have worked with over the last seven years were not entirely happy as full-time mothers. The *Lancet* reports an astonishingly high proportion of depression complaints among mothers. Given that most mothers are alone with their babies for the major part of the day, the best thing we can do is give them *information*. The discovery of capacity in her baby can transform the mother's attitude to the baby. Information is not the same as prescription. As yet we do not know nearly enough about development to offer prescription."

Anneliese Korner, Ph. D.

Maternal Rhythms and Waterbeds: A Form of Intervention with Premature Infants

New medical techniques have dramatically increased the survival rates of premature babies. Now, a growing number of researchers are tackling the more difficult problem of how to help such babies not merely to survive, but to thrive. At issue is the question of whether, and to what extent, extra stimulation can enhance their developmental progress.

Although there seems to be little question about the overriding importance of brain maturation in governing behavioral development, there is a dawning realization that the uneven development so characteristic of premature babies may be due in part to the peculiar environment in which these babies spend their early days. Robbed of weeks or months of the richly nuturing intrauterine environment and the stimulation provided by maternal rhythms and movements, premature babies must make an abrupt and sometimes harsh transition from womb to life—a transition that is often made more difficult by prevailing notions of what constitutes good medical care. Until recently, for example, it was thought advisable to handle premature babies as little as possible in order to avoid the dangers of infection; whatever they received in the way of stimulation was largely limited to stressful medical procedures. The intensive-care nursery, with its lack of patterned stimulation, its continuous bright lights, and the monotonous, loud white noise generated by the incubator motor and other equipment, has been alternately described as an environment of sensory deprivation and sensory bombardment—and a good case can be made for both assertions.

While nothing is known about how premature infants deal with either sensory deprivation or sensory overload, it is clear from studies with adults that both under- and over-stimulation have a disruptive and disorganizing effect on physiological and psychological functioning.

Psychologist Anneliese Korner of the Stanford University Medical School, one of the foremost researchers in this emerging field, is convinced that there is much room for improvement in the nursery environment, particularly in the area of providing more patterned stimulation that isn't linked to intrusive medical procedures. Korner has designed a series of intervention studies aimed not at accelerating development per se, but at creating conditions in which the infant's maturation can progress naturally with a minimum of interference. "Mine is a model," she says, "to offset certain deficits within the environment in which premature infants are currently cared for and to compensate for certain forms of stimulation which are highly prevalent *in utero*...."

For Korner, the purpose of intervention is not to raise developmental quotients measurable months or years after the infant is released from the hospital, but to produce a child who is as intact as possible and therefore better able to cope with whatever home environment he may enter. "What may count the most," says Korner, "is what gets set in motion between parent and child and ... what the infant presents to the parent by way of robustness and intactness is an important factor in this equation."

Since there is ample evidence that pre-term babies do not function as full-term babies do, either psychophysiologically or neurologically, some forms of stimulation to which full-term infants are highly responsive have little relevance for premature infants. A case in point is the pre-term infant's apparent inability to profit much from visual experience—presumably because of an immature nervous system. Likewise, pre-term infants do not seem to respond to social stimulation. Though early interaction with her baby greatly facilitates maternal attachment, such interaction appears to have little direct effect on the infant.

For Anneliese Korner, the key issue was to discover what sort of stimulation might be most relevant and appropriate for premature babies, given their level of neurophysiologic development. Studies of prenatal life have shown that the fetus responds earliest to tactile and vestibular-proprioceptive (the sensation of movement and the sense of position) stimulation. Because child care

practices have emphasized the importance of contact and touch for the early development of young infants, many intervention studies with premature babies have used tactile stimulation, though as Korner points out, when infants are touched, they are almost moved in the process as well.

In Korner's view, there is a strong rationale for providing vestibular-proprioceptive stimulation to small premature babies. For one thing, it's notably lacking in incubators and intensive-care nurseries. More importantly, it's a kind of stimulation richly provided *in utero* by the swirling movements of the amniotic fluid; the postural changes of the mother as she walks, sits, bends, and moves about; and by the movements of the fetal body itself.

Korner's interest in providing compensatory vestibular-proprioceptive stimulation to premature babies grew directly out of more than a decade of developmental research with normal neonates. In the context of this research, she confirmed, not surprisingly, that one of the most effective ways to soothe a crying newborn is to pick the baby up and put him to the shoulder. What *was* surprising to Korner, however, was that the picking babies up in this way, in addition to calming them promptly, almost invariably made them bright-eyed and alert, so that they would begin to scan the environment. "The reason we got excited about this observation," says Korner, "was that it predictably produced a state which many investigators of newborns feel to be the one most conducive to the earliest forms of learning. It is through visual exploration that the infant, lacking motor abilities, is most apt to get acquainted with his environment, including his mother."

Korner and her colleagues then became curious as to what exactly produced the soothing effect and encouraged visual exploration— whether it was mostly body contact, which is usually considered so important, or whether it was motion and the activation of anti-gravity reflexes. To answer this question, Korner tested body contact and vestibular-proprioceptive stimulation for their ability both to soothe and to evoke visual alertness in infants, with and without the upright position.

The results clearly indicated that motion elicited significantly; more visual alertness than did touch alone, and was also more soothing. Further studies, aimed at clarifying the relative efficacy of movement versus the upright position, confirmed that it was the vestibular-proprioceptive stimulation rather than simply being in an upright position that brought about the infant's attentiveness to the environment.

In the process of carrying out these studies, Korner and her colleagues came to appreciate more keenly the role of the vestibular system of the inner ear and the brain in growth and development, and led them to postulate that vestibular-proprioceptive stimulation might be one of the most critical forms of early stimulation for infants. They also discovered that vestibular dysfunction is implicated in some of the most severe developmental deviations. It has been cited as an important factor in the development of dyslexia and other learning disorders, and as a contributing factor in schizophrenia and infantile autism. Studies of

schizophrenic children, for example, have noted the prevalence of vertigo and self-rocking and twirling in such children. Other studies have suggested that *deprivation* of vestibular-proprioceptive stimulation may impair the early development of the brain and its integrating capacities.

What ultimately emerged from all these developmental studies was an ingenious notion: to equip incubators with waterbeds instead of the standard foam rubber mattresses. The waterbeds seemed to Korner not only a naturalistic way of providing vestibular-proprioceptive stimulation to premature infants, but she thought they might have a number of clinical benefits as well, such as helping to preserve the fragile skin of very small infants, and possibly reducing the incidence of their developing asymmetrically shaped heads. Korner designed two types of waterbeds, which have been in use for the past four years. The basic waterbed cradles the infant and is highly responsive to each of his movements. The second type of waterbed is identical in design and consistency, but in addition to the stimulation generated by the infant's own movements, it provides gentle oscillations to ensure that even the most inactive babies are exposed to some motion.

The basic waterbed consists of a high-impact styrene shell and a vinyl bag covered by a latex membrane in a stainless steel frame which attaches to the top of the shell. This unit fits into the incubator to replace the mattress. The temperature of the waterbed is entirely maintained by the incubator's own heating system. When a waterbed is prepared, the vinyl bag is filled with two and a quarter gallons of warm tap water treated with algecide and blue dye. The water temperature chosen is two degrees above the incubator's environmental temperature, since thermal tests have shown that the water temperature stabilizes at that level. The blue dye in the water is designed to alert the hospital staff in case of a leak, which, according to Korner, has occurred only once in four years. Repeated cultures of the water inside the vinyl bag have been negative even after continuous use for more than a month. The frame of the bed provides anchor points to restrain the infant if necessary, and a plastic-covered styroform wedge attached to the frame provides a stable surface to be used whenever it is needed.

In designing the oscillating waterbed, Korner and her colleagues had to decide on the wave form, the rise time, the frequency, and the amplitude of the oscillations. Insofar as possible, Korner tried to avoid completely arbitrary decisions. Instead, she says, "I attempted to make choices which I felt had some clinical, experiential, or biological rationale." First she decided that the oscillations should move in a head-to-foot direction in order to aid the infant's respiratory effort; clinical considerations determined that the oscillations should have a very gentle, barely visible amplitude. To make these very small oscillations more perceptible to the infant, Korner chose a wave with a rise time of half a second. This produces a very gentle jolt that sets the wave in motion, followed by a period of quiescence during which the wave attenuates.

In deciding on the *frequency* of the oscillations, the possibilities were limitless. Here, Korner looked for a biologically relevant rhythm. "I felt

that it would be safest," Korner explains, "to provide a maternal rhythm, since such a rhythm would probably not interfere with the developing organization of the infant's own rhythms and would, at the same time, expose the infant to a rhythm to which he would have been exposed anyway, had he not been born prematurely. The rhythm of maternal respirations in the third trimester of pregnancy is such an experientially relevant rhythm." Thus, the oscillations occur at slightly irregular intervals, at a frequency of 12 to 13 times a minute.

Since waterbeds change the infant's environment on a 24-hour basis, Korner's first study was designed principally to demonstrate their safety. Twenty-one infants ranging in gestational age from 27 to 34 weeks and with birth weights of from 1050 to 1920 grams were randomly assigned to experimental and control groups. The ten babies in the experimental group were placed on the waterbeds before the sixth postnatal day, and remained there for seven days and nights. Their clinical progress was compared with that of a control group of 11 similar babies.

The oscillating waterbed was found to be extremely safe, not affecting any of the infants' vital signs, weight changes, or oxygen requirements. Nor did the waterbed appear to increase the frequency of vomiting. There was, however, one highly significant difference between the two groups, and that was in the incidence of apnea (a temporary cessation of breathing, which is quite common among premature babies). Infants on the oscillating waterbed had far fewer such breathing problems.

A second study in which infants with symptoms of apnea were selected confirmed the finding that apnea is significantly reduced on the oscillating waterbed. In this study Korner used 24-hour polygraphic recordings, with each infant serving as its own control, on and off the waterbeds during alternate six-hour periods. In these two studies, it should be noted, continuous irregular oscillations were used, in the rhythm of maternal respirations, with encouraging clinical results.

Since then, Korner has come to believe that intermittent, rather than continuous, oscillations may be far more effective for developmental purposes, because intermittent stimulation provides periods of both rest and activity, which are probably equally important for the infant's well-being. Again, Korner's rationale is based on a maternal rhythm: the basic rest–activity cycle, which in the adult averages 90 minutes. Korner notes that "maternal cycles exert a regulatory influence on fetal behavior. The prematurely born infant is clearly deprived of [this] potentially organizing influence. The lack of exposure to the maternal cyclicity of physiological and motor activity and rest may very well be one of the contributing factors to the poor organization of sleep seen in premature infants." By superimposing a 90-minute cycle on premature infants (consisting of 30 minutes of oscillations and 60 minutes of quiet), Korner hopes to provide an external aid to the infant's own developing rest–activity cycles. She has just embarked on a developmental, longitudinal study with premature infants in which she is using the intermittent oscillations described above.

Although the long-range developmental effects of the waterbed remain to be seen, their clinical advantages are numerous. They have been used both briefly, to relieve acute conditions, and for as long as three months with some babies. The nonoscillating waterbed has been found particularly beneficial for infants recovering from abdominal surgery and, just as Korner predicted, it helps protect the fragile skin of small infants.

"In watching infants on the waterbed," says Korner, "we have the subjective impression that their motility is more modulated and less random. There seem to be fewer overshooting movements of the limbs, fewer jerks and startles. The infants seem to be better able to establish hand-mouth contact. It is as if the slight containment provided by the waterbeds, as well as possibly the relaxation which attends waterbed flotation, have a binding or organizing effect on the infants' motility."

Lewis P. Lipsitt, Ph. D.

The Pleasures and Annoyances of Infants: Approach and Avoidance Behavior of Babies

To even the most casual observer, it is abundantly clear that the human infant experiences various events in the world as either pleasant or unpleasant. The characteristic attitude of most scientists, however, has been that such mentalistic attributes as pleasure and displeasure have no place in a scientific explanation of the mechanisms by which behavior is elicited or maintained. Nonetheless, Lewis P. Lipsitt of Brown University is at least one well-known psychologist who is not happy about "shunning the question of joy" altogether. "When you hear a baby cry furiously," says Lipsitt, "you know that this is not a state in which he wishes to remain, and you know that the baby will readily learn responses that will reduce the unhappy condition and terminate the cry. Similarly, when we watch a newborn actively rooting in response to a light touch near the mouth, quickly zeroing in on the apparently attractive object, then latching on and sucking it avidly, we are aware that there is pleasure going on in there."

According to Lipsitt, the pleasures and pains of sensation are immediately operative in the newborn, and the experience of enjoyment or annoyance (or some mixture of the two) serves as a kind of screening mechanism through which sensory stimuli pass and are either "appreciated and perpetuated, or censored and expelled." Lipsitt believes, in other words, that newborns engage in systematic congenital patterns of behavior from the earliest moments after birth. These behavior patterns are mediated in part by "hedonic mechanisms" that screen stimulation so that either "further approach behavior ensues or defensive reactions supervene."

Lipsitt outlines a plausible case for the idea that part of the function of early infancy is to provide a period during which the baby receives a fair range of both pleasant and unpleasant experiences, and can rehearse his "congenital response repertoire in relative safety." He further speculates that the first two months of life provide, in effect, a period during which the infant can practice the reflexive behaviors that later (between two and six months of age) become voluntary and operantly guided.

In order to demonstrate the effects of pleasure (or displeasure) on the newborn's subsequent behavior, as well as on his various psychophysiological processes—such as heart rate—Lipsitt and his colleagues have taken advantage of recent advances in polygraphic recording techniques "to document the way in which sensory stimulation, specifically taste, serves to alter what might be called the basic congenital responsivity of the infant."

In a series of studies that focused on sucking and heart rate, Lipsitt and a team of co-workers devised a rather ingenious experimental arrangement. Testing was done in a special crib in which both light and sound could be controlled. Electrodes were placed on the infant's chest and leg, permitting polygraphic monitoring of the primary heart rate. Sucking was recorded on another polygraph channel. The "suckometer" consists of a pressure transducer over which a commercial nipple is pulled. A tube, running into the nipple from a pump source, delivers tiny amounts of fluid activated either by the experimenter or a "suck" of sufficient force. The experimental apparatus could be arranged so that when the infant sucked, he sometimes received no fluid. At other times, with each suck he got one (or more) drops of a fluid such as sugar water, in whatever concentration the experimenter desired.

Newborns, it has been found, characteristically suck in rapid bursts, interspersed with rests. Working with two - and three-day old infants, Lipsitt and his colleagues discovered that the length of these bursts and rests, as well as the sucking rate within bursts, may be importantly influenced by the relative enjoyment derived from sucking. Moreover, variations in these sucking-response parameters relate consistently to one another and to variations in heart rate. For example, the researchers found that with a change from a no-fluid condition to a fluid-sucking condition, or with a change from sucking for a less sweet to a sweeter solution, there is a tendency for the sucking bursts to become longer, for the inter-burst intervals to become

shorter, and for the sucking rate within bursts to become slower.

In one study, Lipsitt observed the sucking behavior of newborns over four successive five-minute periods. The infants received one of five reinforcement regimens. One group received only sucrose; a second group, only plain, distilled water; and a third group received no fluid reinforcement throughout the 20-minute testing period. The fourth group received sucrose and water alternated twice, in five-minute units, and the final group received sucrose alternated with no fluid. Comparing the first three groups, Lipsitt found that the sucking rate within bursts slowed progressively as the infants sucked for nothing, for plain water, or for a 15 percent sucrose solution. Thus, as the apparent incentive value of the reinforcement increases, the sucking response becomes slower and more deliberate. At the same time, however, when the infants sucked for sweet fluids, they tended to take shorter rests than when they sucked for either water or for no fluid. The result, according to Lipsitt, is that despite the slower sucking rate within bursts, the infants actually sucked more times per minute when their behavior was reinforced with a sucrose solution than when it was reinforced with water or not reinforced by any fluid at all.

Lipsitt suggests that this response pattern reflects the pleasure associated with the taste of sweeter fluids. Infants not only suck more consistently for such fluids, they also suck more slowly, "as if to savor them more."

In the groups in which reinforcement conditions were alternated, it was found that the sucking rate also showed reliable alternations that were consistent with the results from the first three groups. More importantly, there was an obvious indication of an experiential effect in these groups. When sucking for sucrose, the response rate of these infants was comparable to that of the infants who received sucrose throughout the testing period. When switched to water or no-fluid, however, their response rate was significantly lower than that of their counterpart controls in the water-throughout and no-fluid-throughout groups. "When newborns have experience in sucking for sucrose," says Lipsitt, "an immediately subsequent experience with water [or no fluid, as the case may be] 'turns them off.' " This negative contrast effect indicates that the behavior of newborns is clearly influenced by experiences that have occurred within the immediately preceding five minutes. The implication is that memory processes are already at work in the newborn, leaving a strong impression, though of an admittedly unknown duration, of the experience just endured. Nonetheless, as Lipsitt notes, "these are the beginnings of learning processes."

The above findings have been replicated in several studies by Lipsitt and his colleagues. In addition, they have uncovered an interesting relationship between the sucking response and heart rate. Under a no-fluid sucking condition, the mean heart rate of the infant is significantly higher than it is when he is resting. In turn, the mean heart rate under sucrose sucking is higher than under the no-fluid condition. Thus, "although the sucking rate within bursts is *reduced* when the infant

sucks for sucrose, heart rate nevertheless increases reliably."

A further experiment, in which the amount of the fluid rather than the sweetness was varied, corroborated these findings. In this study, sweetness was held constant (at a ten percent sucrose concentration) but the amount of fluid for which the babies sucked differed. In some instances, the babies received a .01 ml drop per suck, and in other instances a .03 ml drop. "To our own pleasure," says Lipsitt, "the functional relationships that had been previously established for sweetness held also for amount, for both sucking behavior and heart rate."

Lipsitt contends that a possible interpretation of these effects must include a "hedonic explanation suggesting that sucking rate is modulated to facilitate savoring" of pleasurable experiences. More generally, he notes that these findings point up "the fine interplay between the various congenital responses of the newborn and the extent to which his behavior and psychophysiological indices are affected by the environment." In Lipsitt's view, this work suggests that the relationship between infant and environment is a complex one involving a "constant reciprocity between the infant and the caretaker, in which each serves as stimulus and each responds," and with both operating according to yet-to-be discovered motivational principles.

In a more directly practical vein, Lipsitt points out the potential diagnostic significance of these techniques, as well as the results that they have yielded so far. To the extent that such normative findings can be employed to assess "response deviation" in individual infants, these psychophysiological measures might prove useful in tagging what Lipsitt calls the "deviant newborn." Lipsitt emphasizes that longitudinal studies will be required to determine the long-term usefulness of such neonatal measures as sucking and heart rate for prognostic purposes. But he adds that "with empirical luck, we might be able some day to identify, then intensify our remedial efforts on behalf of, infants with aberrations or deficits for which compensatory training techniques are either now available or will be later."

Although Lipsitt's work has primarily emphasized the "savoring behaviors" of the newborn, he notes that it should be counterbalanced by an acknowledgement of the infant's capacity for what might be termed "negative hedonics," that is, the newborn's evident distaste for certain types of stimulation. This can be readily observed, says Lipsitt, "in the frowning and crying behavior of the baby when he is subjected to very loud noises or other sudden stimulation, such as the rapid onset of a bright light, a pinprick in the heel, or other apparently noxious environmental input." Lipsitt notes that aversive behavior in very young babies has been systematically documented. In one study, the sucking apparatus previously described was adapted to deliver fluid only on demand of the experimenter, not made contingent on the baby's sucking. While infants sucked under a no-fluid condition, the experimenter administered drops of either a salt or a sugar solution during the inter-burst intervals. The times between the administration of fluid drop, the onset of the next sucking burst, as

well as the length of the subsequent burst, was recorded. Not only was the salt solution found to have reliable effects on the infants' sucking behavior, but these effects mirrored those obtained when a sugar concentration was used.

Lipsitt goes beyond the available experimental evidence to comment in a speculative and theoretical way on aversive behavior in the newborn; that is, the infant's reaction to "unpleasant" situations. Defining anger in terms of "the presence and vigor of autonomic and withdrawal responses to noxious stimulation," he suggests that angry behavior does occur in the newborn and serves as the basis for subsequent aggressive behavior in older infants and young children. In his view, aggressive behavior might be considered to derive from defensive responses of the baby that basically serve to put an end to unpleasant stimulation.

For example, a particularly striking pattern of aversive behavior can be seen in the infant's response to the threat of suffocation. Stimulation associated with this threat tends to elicit a kind of fixed action pattern that involves the following five steps: 1) side-to-side head waving; 2) facial vasodilation; 3) head withdrawal, with backward jerks and grimacing; 4) arm jabbing; and 5) crying. This continuum of responses, which Lipsitt regards as angry behavior, often occurs in the course of infant feeding and has the effect of freeing the respiratory passages, either by displacing the offending object or by causing the mother to alter her feeding position.

Because it does lead to a freeing from occlusion, the probability that this "angry reaction" may recur under the same or similar conditions may be increased. The response may subsequently occur with a shorter latency, or simply with the anticipation of its occurrence. Eventually, such "aggressive behaviors" may, in fact, come to be mediated by anger generated under entirely different circumstances. "Initially," says Lipsitt, "a congenital response pattern (anger) is elicited by experiential circumstances conducive to its expression. Components of that action pattern are selectively reinforced, following which, these behaviors (now called aggressive), are learned and perpetuated through reinforcement consequences."

Essentially, Lipsitt is proposing that aggressive behavior is acquired through the same learning mechanisms presumably implicated in other forms of instrumental learning. While Lipsitt's position is largely speculative, as he himself admits, it is clear that the type of aversive behavior he describes warrants more intensive study than it has had until now.

Hanuš Papoušek, M.D.

The Infant's Fundamental Adaptive Response System in Social Interaction

Drs. Hanuš and Mechthild Papoušek, of the Max Planck Institute for Psychiatry in Munich, have long been interested in the development of adaptive behavioral processes in human infants. Although Hanuš Papoušek employed conditioning designs (both operant and Pavlovian) in his former studies, his concern with "the ecological aspects of development and particularly ... the infant's natural interactions with his biological and social environments," has led him to expand upon traditional procedures, supplementing learning data with various forms of physiological and observational data. As a result, the Papoušeks now have been able to obtain a wealth of new information concerning the interrelationship between learning and changes in behavioral state, and have discovered "parallels between experimental learning, play activities, and social interactions."

The Papoušeks believe that a fundamental regulatory system underlies the various categories of adaptive behavior. In other words, such processes as attention, perception, and the organization of other responses are intimately linked. Although other scientists have developed separate models for these processes, the Papoušeks prefer to view them in their "natural unity." Such a conceptually complex approach may be particularly appropriate for the study of infants, who still "talk with the whole body." Since the behaviors of newborns are more limited and, therefore, more predictable than those of older children and adults, the testing and verification of unified psychological models should be greatly facilitated by using neonates.

Two main aspects of the regulatory system proposed by the Papoušeks are the perceptual processing of information and the organization of adaptive responses. To begin with, perception is a complex and active process that is dependent upon innate capacities, past experience, the behavioral state of the infant, and the nature of the information being processed. In addition, the perceiving person may respond to environmental stimulation with changes that, in turn, influence subsequent perceptions; for example, with increased attention or a search for more information.

In his study of the infant's perceptual processes, Hanuš Papoušek employed an instrumental conditioning procedure. After hearing an auditory signal, the infant was required to turn his head in a given direction in order to receive a portion of milk. Papoušek found that within the first week of life, infants were able to learn the appropriate head movement, thus demonstrating an ability "to detect the relationship between their own motor activity and a nutritional reinforcement." By four months of age, they were capable of executing a fairly lengthy series of head movements to obtain reinforcement. Although newborns can learn such instrumental relationships fairly easily, however, it isn't until later in life that they can cope with associative conditioning.

Hanuš Papoušek attributes this fact to "the particular power of contingent stimulation in structuring perception." Evidence for such structuring may be seen in the relationship between orienting responses and contingency. When colored light displays are presented randomly, the infant habituates to the display in 8 to 12 exposures, and all orienting responses drop out. If presentation is made contingent on a head movement, however, the display will elicit much more attention and exploration. In such a case, orienting behavior is resistant to habituation, even after 30 to 40 exposures.

An interesting example of the operation of two different perceptual processes was uncovered by the Papoušeks in a study of five-month-old infants' responses to a mirror. Using television monitors, they simultaneously presented their infants with: 1) a mirror-image of themselves, which precluded eye contact, and 2) a comparable playback of themselves, which allowed eye contact. Both the contingency of behavior seen in the mirror-image, and the eye contact offered by the playback, appeared to be determinants of perception.

However, the latter was detected rapidly and, initially, was preferred by the infants. Only as they gradually discovered the contingency in the behavior of their mirror-image did they begin to pay increasing attention to it and to decrease the attention given the eye-contact image.

These observations led the Papoušeks to categorize environmental events with respect to the infant's adaptive processes as follows:

a) Random external changes. These elicit attention, which habituates rapidly.

b) External changes that are independent of the infant's activity but regularly associated with another relevant change (e.g., food presentation). Once these are detected as "signals," the infant may show intensive orientation toward such changes, and learn to respond in their presence.

c) External changes contingent on the infant's own activity. These elicit the most intensive orienting reactions, which are highly resistant to habituation.

d) Contingent external change where the contingency is difficult to perceive. This presents a problem situation to the infant, and, depending on his maturity and experience, it may either be solved or reacted to as if the changes were random.

The organization of responses is the other aspect of behavioral adaptation with which the Papoušeks have been concerned. The usual approach to the analysis of adaptive behavior has been to consider only observable responses and to attempt to classify them as either genetic in origin, or as learned. This is an oversimplification of behavioral structure, the Papoušeks believe. Even at the level of motor activity, "a vast number of simple elements are integrated into functional units of higher orders," resulting in a hierarchically structured system that encompasses both the reflexes of single muscles and complex motor coordinations such as those involved in locomotion. Beyond this, adaptive behaviors may entail more than just specific motor responses to stimulation. They also involve attentional and perceptual processes as well as memory, exploration, and decision-making. Finally, they may include such nonspecific responses as changes in the autonomic system which provide the energy supply and metabolic adjustments necessary to enable the infant to react to external stimuli in an adaptive manner.

While at times the organization of adaptive responses may involve the relatively straight-forward structuring of unconditioned reflexes, it can, at other times, involve learning or cognitive processes, as in a problem situation involving the detection of a complex form of contingency.

There are two important features in the Papoušeks' description of the organization of adaptive responses. First, they see the adaptive system as including not only particular responses which are appropriate to relevant biological demands (e.g., hunger or pain), but also more general responses which act to facilitate the regulation of informational input and information processing. Secondly, they view these fundamental adaptive responses, including many cognitive processes, "almost as a category of unconditioned responses." Indeed, if

one were to think of the Papoušeks' formulation in terms of drive theory, the fundamental adaptive response system could be classified as a basic drive, participating in all other categories of drives. In order to respond to any biologically relevant situation, the organism "first has to activate the mechanisms controlling informational input and processing and all subsequent cognitive or learning processes up to the evaluation of the final outcome."

The presence and significance of general adaptive responses is particularly obvious in human infants, where such responses occur slowly and are manifested in the total motor behavior. In newborns, the Papoušeks have been able to observe "the activation of orienting responses, the gradual organization of individual components of a newly learned response, and the participation of autonomic and communicative changes in behavioral states." In older infants, the organization of more complex, rule-governed behavior patterns has been studied.

In the course of this work, the Papoušeks were particularly struck by the amount of effort that infants seemed willing to exert in order to find solutions to problematical learning situations. This, of course, raised the question of underlying motivation, for, says Papoušek, "the efforts of the infants sometimes seemed to threaten them with exhaustion." Surprisingly, motivation seemed to be independent of hunger in those experiments in which milk served as a reinforcer. Even as the infant became satiated, to the point of refusing to drink, conditioning signals continued to elicit quick, intensive, and correct head movements and signs of obvious pleasure. Similarly, when head turns were rewarded by displays of colored lights, infants appeared to gradually lose interest in the display itself, observing other things during its presentation, while at the same time continuing to perform the response necessary to activate the display. They did, however, become upset if the reinforcements were omitted.

It seems that "the infant expects a certain result to follow from his motor act, and the congruency between his expectation and the real outcome pleases him, whereas an incongruency upsets him and elicits new exploration." In short, the performance of a correct adaptive response may motivate the infant more strongly than such external reinforcers as food or visual stimulation."

Some theories of motivation have tended to stress incongruency or dissonance as the primary motivational factor. The Papoušeks' observations of infant behavior suggest, however, that genuinely pleasurable experiences result from the outcome of the baby's fundamental adaptive processes. Consequently, they believe that infants "may be as strongly pulled by the expectation of pleasure connected with successful adaptation as they are pushed by unpleasant feelings resulting from incongruency, dissonance, or failure in adjustment."

The fundamental adaptive response system proposed by the Papoušeks encompasses several different response patterns. From the point of view of stimulus-response theory, what they refer to as fundamental adaptive responses represent mediating or intervening variables. In the absence of neurophysiological evidence for the anatomical unity of such a system, the Papoušeks emphasize the unity represented by the inter-relationships among its individual parts. They assume that these relationships are probabilistic and bi-directional. An example of such dynamic interaction may be seen in the relationship between behavioral state and measures of learning. Not only may the behavioral state preceding a conditioning signal influence the course of the learned response, but, conversely, the course of learning may affect subsequent behavioral states.

In effect, the Papoušeks expand the traditional conception of the stimulus-response relationship to encompass two additional concepts: information processing and the organization of adaptive responses. Moreover, they emphasize that all of these interact with (that is, exert mutual influence on) one another. The mechanisms regulating informaion processing and response organization are assumed by the Papoušeks to be two-fold. These processes may be either positively activated (leading to approach and exploration), or actively inhibited (leading to avoidance).

The Papoušeks consider the inhibition of the adaptive response system to play an important role in protecting infants against floods of information, especially information that is difficult to process. For example, they found that avoidance-like responses, such as turning the head away, occur frequently when infants are confronted with relatively difficult problem-solving situations. In addition, they noted a developmental change in the form of reduction of information processing. Infants younger than two months typically respond to difficult problem-solving situations with a temporary change to a quiescent behavioral state characterized by a lack of convergence of the eyes and slowing down of respiration and heartbeat. It is almost as if they are "playing possum." On the other hand, older infants tend to respond with an active redistribution of interest, without necessarily changing their behavioral state.

In summary, the Papoušeks conceptualize the adaptive response system as "a complex set of processes concerned with the regulation of behavioral states, attention, perception, memory, orienting, exploration, learning, and cognition." This system consists of unconditioned responses to external stimuli as well as to the internal products which result from the processing of those stimuli. It serves to integrate the internal products in different forms of learning, from simple habituation through complex concept formation. Finally, it may operate to either activate or inhibit analytic and integrative mechanisms in accordance with the adaptive needs of the organism. The motivation for the adaptive response system is assumed to derive from "mediating" outcomes within the nervous system, which include a kind of intrinsic "reward" or punishment" in the form of the pleasant or unpleasant" feelings, arising from successful or unsuccessful adaptation.

The Papoušeks, apart from their theoretical formulations, have been intensely interested in establishing a link between laboratory situations and natural learning situations. Therefore, they determined to explore the implications that their concept of fundamental adaptive responses might have for our understanding of both play and social interaction.

The biological meaning of (as well as the motivation for) play behavior has long presented a problem for theorists. The Papoušeks attempt to approach this problem from the point of view of fundamental adaptive responses. Cognitive processes represent a movement from "unknown" to "known." This movement should not, however, exceed certain limits; too much uncertainty elicits fear or stress, while too little results in boredom. There are two complementary strategies involved in the adaptive process which direct such movement. The first tends to integrate information into a complete and closed concept. The second tends to open seemingly complete concepts, bringing them into unexpected new relations, and, essentially, making the "known" more "unknown" again. The Papoušeks feel that this second strategy is not only involved in play, but is essential to the creative arts and to humor as well.

According to this approach, "play can only start at the point where a certain amount of integrated knowledge has already been accumulated." Thus play would not be possible at the beginning of postnatal life. Interestingly, parental behavior during this very early period may, through its timing and repetitious nature, provide the infant with stimulation that compensates for his lack of playful or creative activities. Specifically, the Papoušeks note that parents repeat behavioral patterns until they begin to cease to elicit much attention, and then suddenly modify them, adding surprising new elements. In this way, the infant learns to recognize a given event and at the same time, to expect changes which increase the attractiveness of that event. He may, in fact, be learning how to prevent boredom through "play."

The tendency of parents to repeat and exaggerate behavioral patterns also clearly facilitates the infant's cognitive development, the Papoušeks note. The parent's ability to allocate, and time stimulation, is especially important during the early months of life, when the infant's behavioral state fluctuates frequently and irregularly. The Papoušeks have found that the mother in interactions with her child, evaluates the infant's behavioral state, attempts to maintain it at an optimal level, and decides on the basis of the infant's attention, whether to continue or modify her repetitive stimulation. Among the primary cues she utilizes are visual contact, facial expression, muscle tone, and vocalizations. It is through this activity on the part of the mother that the infant's adaptive responses come to guide subsequent maternal behavior.

A final characteristic of parental behavior which may play an important role in the infant's cognitive development is the tendency of parents to imitate the baby's facial expressions, vocalizations, and movements. From the very beginning of life, parents provide infants with a kind of "biological mirror." The Papoušeks believe that this activity enables the infant to "associate his interoceptive information about his own movements with their visual representation." They further suggest that this may be the first step toward the development of self-awareness and personal identity.

Above all, the Papoušeks stress, "the social interaction between the infant and an adult caretaker consists of a great number of natural learning situations in which the fundamental adaptive processes in the infant play a major role." These processes, it is important to note, elicit responses in the mother, providing her with feedback information that enables her to pattern her own behavior in an optimal way. In short, the responses described by the Papoušeks as the "fundamental adaptive system" clearly facilitate and accentuate the processes of learning and cognition in the infant, and are important in keeping the mother-infant system integrated for the infant's survival. Their further study will doubtless yield a far better understanding of the early regulation of infant behavior.

William Mason, Ph.D.

Maternal Deprivation: Biological and Evolutionary Perspectives

The development of cognitive skills is closely related to the gratification of basic emotional needs and motivational drives. This is true for virtually all species, throughout the life cycle. But the interplay betwen what might be called "wanting" and "knowing" is nowhere more evident than in the developing relationship between parent and young. Cognitive and motivational elements are closely interwoven from the very beginning of this relationship, and their interdependence is partly what is meant when maternal patterns or filial responses are referred to as "instinctive."

For many species, the interplay between wanting and knowing in the parent-offspring relationship has implications that go far beyond the giving and receiving of care necessary for the immediate survival of the offspring. The parent, for example, is often described as "teacher" or "model" or "socializer", words which refer to the parent's effects not on the offspring's immediate survival, but on its long-range prospects. The relationship between parent and offspring, in other words, serves as an important model; it foreshadows not only future social relations, but the infant's later relations with the whole environment. In this sense it is a pivotal relationship, for it includes those things that are peculiar to the conditions and requirements of infancy, plus elements that are representative of the larger world.

For William A. Mason, a psychologist at the California Primate Research Center and the Davis campus of the University of California, it is this combination of specialized and generalized features that make the mother-infant relationship so intriguing an object of study. Mason's work is with nonhuman primates, and the subject of most of his research is the developing rhesus monkey. He has experimented with various forms of intervention in the natural mother-infant relationship in order to examine the developmental consequences. For Mason, the interesting question is not *whether* development will be altered by abnormal circumstances, but *how*. It is his thesis that "one of the most basic and significant consequences of depriving an infant monkey of its natural mother is a disruption of the normal intimate interplay between the processes subserving 'wanting' and 'knowing' which may lead to fundamental changes in the way the infant relates to the world in the later stages of its life."

To illustrate, Mason offers an extreme example: the infant rhesus monkey separated from its mother at birth and raised with a cloth artificial mother. He explains that such a monkey "wants" to cling to something and its early behavior is exquisitely organized to permit it to do so. "The monkey 'knows' from the moment it enters the world what its mother 'feels like'", says Mason, but it does not know specifically how she will look. Consequently, virtually any claspable object, regardless of its appearance, can become the focus of attachment.

"In time the maternal figure becomes known through vision, of course. It is recognized at a distance and from various angles of regard; and its presence becomes a powerful source of emotional security. As a security object—the 'wanting' part of the relationship—an inanimate surrogate may be as effective as the real mother, at least in early developmental stages. What is conspicuously lacking in the relationship with an inanimate surrogate, however, is the presence of those dynamic attributes that facilitate and support the development of knowledge and skill. With an inanimate mother, life is all too easy. A cloth mother holds no surprises; she engenders no conflicts, makes no unexpected demands, sets no conditions, neither placates nor punishes. She is simply there, available and inert."

Mason and his colleagues have found that even a modest increase in the dynamic attributes of an artificial mother, such as mechanizing her so that she moves somewhat unpredictably around the cage, can have lasting effects on an infant's psychological development, including visual curiosity and social behavior. Mason's data indicate that monkeys raised with mobile artificial mothers show both a higher level of visual curisoity and more adequate sexual performance than those raised with stationary mother surrogates.

As Mason points out, however, it is obvious that "a cloth-covered dummy, even a mobile one, is a far cry from a real monkey mother." And so, seeking a closer approximation of the real thing, Mason and his colleagues turned, in the next phase of their research, to canine mother substitutes.

Their current project includes animals raised with either cloth-and-plastic surrogates or with dogs. All the monkeys are housed outdoors with surrogates in spacious kennels that allow for frequent visual contact with people, dogs, and other monkeys. From the third to the fifteenth month of life, every monkey was regularly permitted to roam in several different complex outdoor enclosures containing a variety of playthings, puzzles, and climbing devices. The aim was to provide all monkeys with a generally "enriched" experience, while withholding from some (those raised with cloth surrogates) the opportunity for give and take in a relationship that really mattered—"to separate", as Mason puts it, "the attachment *per se,* from the dynamic (and paradigmatic) properties of the attachment figure."

Dogs were used instead of real mothers for several reasons. "Of particular importance," says Mason, "was our knowledge that dogs were tolerant, accepting, and highly social attachment figures and yet did not display the typical primate-specific patterns of maternal solicitude and restraint." He points out, in fact, that there is no indication that the dogs respond maternally to the monkeys in any way. That is, they don't seem particularly concerned with what the monkey is doing, except as it affects them. Mason characterizes the dogs' relationship to the monkeys as being very much like what you'd expect to find in a household pet in its relations with children in the family: tolerant, but only up to a point. They don't accept abuse; they control, and they are controlled. "The dogs like the monkeys, yes; play with them to be sure; they even growl at them on occasion, particularly as the monkeys grow older and more rambunctious; but on the whole they are remarkably gentle and indulgent. Our hope was that such a 'generalized' companion would as surrogate mother throw more light on the broader effects of social stimulation than would a natural mother, whose behavior has been shaped by evolution to complement, support and direct the development of her offspring along species-typical paths."

The inanimate surrogates used in this research are plastic hobby horses mounted on wheels. They carry a "saddle" of acrylic "fur" to which the infant monkeys can cling. Although the data are not all in, the findings so far do suggest that the monkey's basic stance toward the environment, its characteristic approach to the world is significantly altered by the kind of mother substitute with which it has been raised.

One of the simplest measures taken was the amount of time the monkey spent looking at its surrogate. Not surprisingly, the monkeys raised with dogs spent considerably more time looking at them throughout the first year of life than did the monkeys raised with hobby horses.

When the monkeys were about four months old, the researchers began to test them in a delayed response situation, the reward for a correct

response being contact with the surrogate mother. The most striking difference between the two groups was the higher level of "balks" in the hobby horse group: they simply refused to respond to forty-six percent of the trials, as compared with less than two percent for the dog-raised monkeys.

The researchers also administered a variety of tests in which the monkeys were observed in novel surroundings. In one test, the monkeys were placed in an unfamiliar room on three separate occasions, approximately fifty days apart, starting when they were four months old. On each occasion five test conditions were presented. These included the monkey's surrogate available for contact; the surrogate enclosed in a plastic box (so that it could be seen but not touched); an unfamiliar surrogate (dog or hobby horse, corresponding to rearing group) available for contact and enclosed in the plastic box; and the empty test chamber.

Two results stand out: first, the monkeys raised with inanimate surrogates did not differentiate the social conditions as sharply as did the dog-reared group. Second, when they were alone in the test chamber, their levels of heart rate and distress vocalizations were much lower than those of the monkeys raised with dogs. These results could be taken to indicate that monkeys raised with inanimate surrogates are generally calmer, less susceptible to stress. Mason believes, however, that a more correct interpretation is that the characteristic way of coping with novel situations is vastly different in the two groups. "The monkeys raised with hobby horses," he explains, "surely experienced much less response-contingent feedback in their relations with the attachment figure than did monkeys raised with dogs."

Apparently, the critical factor is that these monkeys failed to learn, in their relations with inanimate surrogates, that the environment could be controlled. Mason explains that for the monkey, "the most significant object in its early life is the mother. If you give it a mother substitute that doesn't do anything, that doesn't make any demands, that doesn't need to be predicted, ... you create an animal whose basic stance towards the environment is altered. The monkey is not curious about what's happening around it. It doesn't act upon the environment in situations where you might expect it to..." Thus, when faced with a novel situation, such as solitary confinement in an unfamiliar room, the monkeys raised with hobby horses were less likely to try to escape or attempt to change their condition than were monkeys raised with dogs; they were more likely to accept the situation passively and therefore were less distressed by it.

Mason has gathered additional data from a number of simple problem-solving tests showing similarly striking contrasts between the two groups in their relations with the environment. One test series began by presenting food in an open box of clear plastic suspended 30 cm above the floor; after thirty trials, this condition was altered by raising the box to 60 cm above the floor and providing a wooden step. The level of successful performance of the monkeys raised with inanimate surrogates was consistently below that of the monkeys raised with dogs.

The researchers were also interested in how visual activity might be affected by rearing conditions. The animals were subjected to a variety of tests in an enclosed room containing peepholes through which they could look at projected color transparencies. In all such tests, the monkeys raised with dogs consistently demonstrated a much higher level of visual curiosity than did the monkeys raised with hobby horses.

On the whole, Mason's results provide a convincing demonstration of the central importance of early social experience to the interrelations between "wanting" and "knowing" in the developing rhesus monkey. Moreover, his studies indicate that merely "enriching" the environment is not enough to override the effects of having a live companion as a mother substitute.

The fact that the attachment figure for some of the monkeys was a dog rather than the natural mother is significant, says Mason, "for it suggests that the critical dimensions in early social life are not closely tied to the highly specific structure of the natural mother-infant relation. This is not to say that the particularities of the natural relation are without influence, of course, but only that they are apparently superimposed on rather generalized developmental systems."

For nonhuman primates, the propensity to form a strong emotional attachment to a maternal figure is a conspicuous and virtually universal characteristic. And "wanting", says Mason, "in the context of filial attachment, leads naturally to an elaboration of those processes subserving 'knowing'." Mason's results give some indication of the different consequences that follow from having an attachment figure that is living or inert. But as he observes, "even when the object of attachment is a cloth dummy, surely not a propitious vehicle for the development of complex cognitive dispositions and skills, 'knowing' processes of a simple order are plainly involved. Such a 'mother' becomes recognized on sight, and the attachment to her is specific and preferential.

"For the nonhuman primates this means that the maternal figure occupies a privileged and influential position, one particularly well-suited to shape the early development of behavior. Is the primate mother unique in this respect? This seems unlikely. Data on a host of species demonstrate the broad range and subtlety of maternal effects. The details vary with species, of course, but the thesis of privileged influence is fully supported by the facts.

"Having given the mother her due, however, it is important to recognize that her effects on development may sometimes reflect sufficient rather than necessary conditions. We need no reminder that the developing individual is neither a lump of clay, passively shaped at the whim of any potter's hand, nor a clock-work automaton with machinery set and ready for entrainment. Once embarked on his brief career, we know that the developing individual plays an active role in all that transpires. He selects from the environment the best that is available to him, as dictated by his existing structure and organization, and he is altered as a consequence of his acts. This is the basic dialogue in which all living systems are endlessly engaged, and it is carried forward at every functional level. While life goes on the dialogue continues in some form, regardless of what the environment offers. Natural mothers, like dogs and dummies, produce their effects as participants in this process."

Leon Yarrow, Ph.D.

Problems in Procedures for Exploring Parent-Infant Interaction

Direct observation of infant behavior and of parent-infant interaction has become an increasingly popular technique of data collection in the past decade. At the same time, although research technology has become more sophisticated, there has been no systematic rationale for the observational methods used. Techniques for observing parents and infants have been developed haphazardly, sometimes dictated by the objectives of a given study, sometimes tied to the conceptual framework of an individual investigator. More often than not, each researcher has developed his or her own system for observing and recording behaviors.

According to psychologist Leon Yarrow, chief of the Social and Behavioral Sciences Branch of the National Institute of Child Health and Human Development, this unsystematic approach leads to difficulties in understanding parent-infant interaction. Yarrow and his colleague Barbara J. Anderson outline three fundamental issues that need to be considered in developing methods for observation. These are: 1) the choice of settings for observing parent and infant behaviors; 2) the choice of categories for indexing parent-infant interaction; and 3) the choice of strategies for sampling behaviors.

Yarrow and Anderson point out that parent-infant interaction has been studied in a variety of settings: in the familiar surroundings of the home, in the unfamiliar laboratory environment, and sometimes in a laboratory setting designed to be like the home. Whether in home or laboratory, observational studies sample behavior in a variety of situations, such as feeding, bathing, and free play. It should go without saying that the behaviors of parents and infants are influenced by both the physical settings and the specific situations in which they are observed, yet research on parent-infant interaction has not attempted to sample behaviors systematically across either settings or situations. It is likely, for example, that a feeding situation elicits quite different behaviors from both parent and infant than a free play situation. Investigators who have separately analyzed feeding and nonfeeding situations as different contexts for maternal and infant behavior have concluded, not surprisingly, that observation of mother-infant transactions in only one context would inevitably result in misleading conclusions.

Moreover, most studies do not take into consideration the parent's view of the situation nor the expectations and biases associated with a given setting. These expectations and biases are influenced by how comfortable the parent feels about being observed, as well as any number of personality characteristics. In the natural setting of the home, even when parents and infants are completely free to do as they wish, their interactions may be influenced in subtle ways. The mere presence of the observer has an effect; and how the purpose of the observation is explained to the parents may distort or mask typical parent-infant exchanges. In addition, some situations, like feeding, may be conflict-ridden for particular parent-infant pairs, while for others feeding may be a very pleasurable experience.

Another influence on both infant and parent behavior is the state of the infant. Although increasing attention has been paid to the infant's state of arousal in laboratory settings, researchers who study infants in the home have rarely monitored the infant's state. The infant's state strongly influences both his own behavior and his mother's response. For example, the infant's responsiveness has a lot to do with how sleepy or alert he is. Cultural differences, also play a role. For example, one investigator studied three-month-old infants and their mothers in Japan and compared them with similar pairs in the United States. He found that infant irritability and sleep states were perceived differently by Japanese and American mothers, and elicited quite different maternal responses.

Yarrow and Anderson observe that "if we analyze the studies on parent-infant interaction and attempt to organize the variables within some framework, we are struck by the many different frames of reference and the many different levels of variables." There are categories for describing simple, observable behavior such as talking, touching, or holding the infant. Some variables cannot be directly observed, but can be derived from combinations of observable behaviors. Still other variables must be inferred; they are based on a great number of cues which the observer must organize and synthesize. An example is the degree to which the mother individualizes the child and is sensitive to his special likes and dislikes and unique characteristics. Often the only way to get at such attitudes or feelings is through ratings made by observers after a long series of observations; sometimes the observations need to be supplemented by interviews.

Yarrow and Anderson emphasize that the research findings of behavioral scientists are very closely influenced by their methods of observation and their analytical techniques. There are several problems related to the choice of contexts in which observations are made, the categories used in observing behavior, and the strategies for sampling and recording behavior.

"With regard to contexts," Yarrow and Anderson note, "investigators have considered the home environment too simply as representing a homogeneous 'natural' situation across families in which one observes behaviors without imposing any constraints. However, on closer examination it is apparent that a variety of dimensions seldom mentioned in the literature influence the extent and quality of interactive behavior observed in the home. It is therefore essential in our research to tap mother-infant interaction in a variety of settings and to analyze separately the behaviors occurring in each setting and under varying degrees of structure. We must begin to look at the demand characteristics of different situations as well as at variations in infant state in an effort to understand the meaning of different contexts to the parent, the infant, and the pair.

"With regard to structure, we should not assume that either a 'free' situation in the natural setting or a controlled one in the laboratory is inherently superior. Each has its advantages and limitations.... The choice of the appropriate combination of structure and setting will depend on the specific research questions we ask. We need methodological studies to help us understand the different kinds of behaviors elicited with differing degrees of structure.

"Many of these contextual influences in the natural setting are not easily identified; sometimes we are not aware of them, often our vague awareness leads us to minimize their importance. We need descriptive data on the characteristics of different contexts as well as studies of the influence of these contexts on parent and infant behavior."

In recent years there has been a tendency to choose "objective" variables and to avoid inferential ones. Studies limited to objective variables have yielded important findings. Nevertheless, Yarrow and Anderson warn that "we must look closely at the meaning of the data we obtain." For example, if during a two-hour home observation one mother is observed touching her infant 23 times and another mother touches her infant 46 times, conclusions from these data should be made only with great caution. "Can

we even be certain," ask the authors, "that, in another two-hour observation, the one mother is more likely to give the infant greater tactile stimulation than the other? If this generalization is possible, what inferences can we make about these two mother-infant relationships? We need to pause and think about the meaning of our simple categories of mother-infant observation."

Yarrow and Anderson stress the importance of examining closely the meaning of the variables used for describing mother-infant interaction. Using the same example, they ask, can we conclude that the infant who receives 46 touches obtains twice the amount of affective stimulation as the baby who got 23?" One infant may, for example, be more sensitive to auditory than to tactile stimulation, and may perceive the same amount of touching very differently from a baby with a lower threshold for tactile stimulation. Similarly, with regard to the mother, Yarrow and Anderson suggest that it may be misleading simply to conclude that the mother who gives more tactile stimulation is more highly stimulating or more responsive or sensitive to the needs of the infant.

Yarrow and Anderson point to similar problems with the more abstract and more subjective variables. For example, even if two observers can obtain adequate reliability in rating an aspect of parent behavior such as respect for the infant's autonomy, a high rating may have different meanings for different mother-infant pairs. For one mother, it may mean she values the infant's need to be independent and encourages it. For another mother, it may mean a reluctance to become engaged with her baby or an exaggerated expectation of what the infant should be able to do for himself, with the result that she attempts to elicit behavior beyond his capabilities. For the baby, it may mean he feels neglected or overstimulated, frustrated, or challenged.

A basic issue in obtaining a representative sample of behavior is the question of day-to-day or hour-to-hour consistency in the behavior of the mother and of the infant. "How much predictability should one expect? We do not know whether the behavior of parent and infant are consistent across time and in different contexts and situations. We do know that there are great daily variations in infant state and individual differences in infants' behavior; we have ignored the relation between consistency in the behavior of the infant and consistency in parental perception of the infant. Parents' behavior may be determined by their image of the infant far more than his actual changing states. Parents as well as infants show individual differences in consistency of behavior."

With regard to recording, Yarrow and Anderson note that "in recording observational data on parent-infant interaction we must make several decisions. First, is the unit of behavior to be a single, discrete response—such as touch, smile, or vocalization—removed from the cluster of responses in which it is embedded? Most observation systems record behavior as though one response occurs in isolation from other responses. Reciprocal social interaction is much more complex.

"Next, is the time aspect of behavior to be recorded, and if so, in what detail? For some behaviors which are momentary—such as burping or early smiling—a concern with onset, duration, and termination of response is not relevant. However, for other behaviors, such as crying or visual attention, we must make decisions concerning the precision with which we record the onset, length, ending and overlap of responses. Inasmuch as the behavioral repertoires of mother and infant are not similar with respect to frequency of occurrence or duration of individual behaviors, there are special problems in recording these time dimensions of behavior. For example, the vocalizations of the mother are more frequent and longer than the infant's early vocalizations, yet accurate assessment of the vocal behavior of both mother and infant is critical if we are to understand the importance of vocal communication in their early relationship."

Another fundamental issue in recording behavior concerns the way in which the observer breaks into the stream of on-going behaviors. This has been done in two ways, by "event sampling" and by "time-dependent sampling." In event sampling, the observer records the frequency of preselected behavior categories as they occur. While the exact frequency of occurrence and possibly the sequence of events may be preserved, it is not possible to analyze the duration of events or the time between behaviors. For sampling that depends on time there are two methods: time-sampling and continuous recording. Each has its own advantages, limitations, and, more importantly, each yields different kinds of data.

Observers who use time-sampling methods look for a set time interval, then record whether one or more predetermined behavioral categories occurred during that interval. Recently, investigators have used relatively short consecutive time-sampling intervals, observing and recording without taking a break. These techniques for indicating the sequence of maternal and infant behavior within short specified intervals give significant information on interaction, in contrast to the techniques that simply record the behavior of one partner in the presence of the other.

Interaction refers strictly to a reciprocal relationship between two or more persons in which the behavior of one person is conditional upon a response from the other and, in turn, the other person's behavior is influenced by the partner's response. Yarrow and Anderson note that until recently, research on mother-infant interaction has ignored the infant's role in eliciting and regulating maternal behavior. To study this reciprocal interaction properly, they believe, one must adopt a systems orientation. Categories to describe parent-infant interaction should consider the behavior of each member of the pair in relation to the behavior of the other.

"If interactional analysis ultimately means characterizing mother and infant as a social system," say the authors, "we need a vocabulary to describe the process. Our standard recording systems are not well-adapted to this purpose. We have categories for describing only the elements of the interaction, not the process itself."

For some purposes, according to Yarrow and Anderson, it may be sufficient simply to record the frequency with which the parent speaks to or cuddles the infant. For some research questions, it may be adequate to know that the infant receives a large amount of verbal stimulation. However, if one does not know whether the infant is listening attentively, babbling back to the mother, or becoming excited or soothed by the mother's verbalizations, then one cannot assume that the infant is receiving the stimulation that is being given.

So-called contingency codes have been used by psychologists to indicate that a behavior of one member of the mother-infant pair follows the behavior of the other member within a specified time interval. Contingency codes preserve the sequence of behaviors but do not distinguish behaviors that follow one another from behaviors that overlap or happen concurrently. These codes, moreover, are restricted to descriptions of brief sequences; they provide no flexibility in describing the repertoire of maternal behaviors that may precede or follow an infant behavior.

Interactional categories which define concurrent mother-infant behavior have been relatively rare because simultaneous behavior is difficult to observe and record in the natural environment, unless one uses film or videotape. The one such category frequently used is mutual visual regard between parent and infant. Studies of mutual regard have documented the predominance of asymmetry between a mother's gaze and that of her infant during the early months of life. The mother provides what has been called a "gaze frame." She continuously looks at the baby while the infant visually cycles in and out, satisfying needs for both interaction and withdrawal.

While categories of concurrence or contingency provide important information and have added to an understanding of parent-infant interaction, they still deal only with the elements of parent-infant exchange.

Parent-infant interaction is a concept that has been honored in name only, Yarrow and Anderson believe. They argue that until recently there has been little recognition of the basic meaning of the concept, and the methods used for studying parents and infants have been inadequate for examining reciprocal chains of relationships. In order to test hypotheses of social reciprocity, according to Yarrow and Anderson, "we must be able to describe the temporal sequencing and clustering of infant and maternal behavior. Recording behavioral interaction requires a methodology which allows one to see how the behavior of one member of the parent-infant pair is significant for the behavior system of the other member. Techniques of continuous recording begin to provide us with a means for recording the process of the interaction and the role of the parent and infant in establishing and maintaining reciprocal exchanges. With further refinements, they should help us obtain data relevant to the theoretical model of mother and infant as a bidirectional system."

Victor H. Denenberg, Ph.D.

Paradigms and Paradoxes in Views of the Infant

Children's development is characterized by rapid and dynamic changes—physical, physiological, and behavioral. Precisely because of these changes, the study of developmental processes poses unique problems and demands different research strategies than the study of the same processes during the relatively stable period of adulthood. University of Connecticut psychobiologist Victor H. Denenberg is one of a growing minority of scientists who have become dissatisfied with some of the standard models used in developmental research. Instead, Denenberg advocates the intensive study of individual units (the infant, the infant-caregiver pair, the family constellation) and the application of the concepts of general systems theory.

The deficiencies of some of the models presently used in developmental research are subtle and insidious, and can lead to contradictory conclusions, Denenberg believes. For example, the simplest kind of experimental design used to study a developmental process consists of an experimental group and a control group, to which subjects have been randomly assigned. At some point early in life, the experimental subjects are given a treatment (the independent variable), followed by a period of time during which all subjects are treated exactly alike. Then, at some point later in life, both groups of subjects are given what is called a "criterion test" on the issue (or dependent variable) under investigation, and the researcher draws conclusions about whether the experimental treatment made the subjects better or worse than the control subjects.

This design is a standard one used in animal studies to evaluate the effects of early experiments. One such experience that has been intensively studied is called handling. A typical procedure is to handle infant animals (usually rats) for three minutes a day for the first twenty days of life, while control animals are left undisturbed. At weaning (twenty-one days) all animals are kept in laboratory cages under constant conditions until later testing, which typically involves an evaluation called the open-field test. The usual finding is that experimental animals are more active and defecate less than animals in the control group. The open-field test is often used as a measure of the construct of emotionality, and a common conclusion, according to Denenberg, is that "handling in infancy brings about a reduction in emotionality...." He observes that such a conclusion is a direct statement about causality, and notes that there is usually an implicit (sometimes explicit) statement to the effect that the less emotional animal is better adapted to its environment, and therefore that handling makes for a "better" animal.

Because it is virtually impossible to control a child's environment totally, most human developmental studies lack the experimental rigor that is possible with animal studies. However, says Denenberg, many researchers have conducted experiments that they interpret *as though* they were working within the experimental design just outlined. He offers the example of one researcher working with a group of babies, who presumably did not receive sufficient "mothering." When compared with a control group, these babies were reported to have a number of psychological and psychiatric disturbances, and some of them even died. The researcher concluded that lack of mothering caused the subsequent psychological disablement or death of the children.

Denenberg cites Operation Headstart as a more recent example of an intervention at the preschool level with subsequent evaluations made in terms of academic achievement measures.

Some of the independent variables that have been studied include the presence or absence of nursery school experience, whether children have had consistent interactions with loving adults or not, and so forth. In a number of these studies, there has been no control group; the subjects are simply compared to some set of population norms.

These examples could be multiplied many times over, says Denenberg. The important point is that this experimental model is the prototype used by many developmental researchers, whether they work with

animals or with humans, whether they have randomly assigned subjects to treatment groups or not, whether they have a control group or not. According to Denenberg, the very structure of the experimental design forces one to draw conclusions that are logically flawed. Thus, the interpretations may be nothing more than artifacts of the model itself, and, what is worse, may have little or nothing to do with the actual nature of the relationships between the independent and dependent variables. Denenberg concedes that there are a number of uses for single variable designs in developmental studies. He emphasizes, however, that "conclusions concerning causality, and value judgements about 'better' or 'poorer' cannot be logically derived from single variable designs because of the extremely high likelihood that experiential and biological variables interact over an organism's developmental life history."

A so-called factorial design, which takes into account the fact that qualitatively different experiences occur at different ages, does allow one to test for causality. Such a design might include three time periods in early life (designed as T1, T2, and T3), with different experimental treatments, or variables, occurring at each interval. For example, T1, T2, and T3 could refer to the first, second, and third years of life respectively. The A variable could indicate whether the baby was breast or bottle fed during the first year; the B variable could indicate whether or not the mother stayed home with her child during the second year; and the C variable could specify whether or not the child went to nursery school during the third year.

The presence of robust main effect and the lack of strong interactions among the variables would justify the conclusion that the variable with the significant main effect is a causal variable . On the other hand, the presence of strong interactions with weak or insignificant main effects would indicate that none of the independent variables, taken alone, has causal consequences. According to Denenberg, only a few variables, even in the more rigorous developmental literature on animals, have been found strong enough to be true causes. A more typical finding is the variables interact with one another across time, and that such interactions result in patterns of experience during early development that yield performance differences in later life. But, says Denenberg, "unless we are willing to extend our definition to think of configurations of experiences over time in a particular context as being 'the cause', the concept of causality becomes meaningless when these kinds of findings are obtained."

In human developmental studies, it is especially clear that qualitatively different experiences at different ages interact with one another rather than adding up neatly into conclusions about causality. Denenberg cautions against discussing developmental phenomena in a causal context at all unless there is very strong evidence that a particular kind of experience (variable) is powerful enough to have similar consequences whenever applied, independent of other intervening experiences.

In addition to the experimental approach, correlational procedures are probably the most widely used techniques in the study of human development. A statement often found in the developmental literature is that some variable measured in early life is not related to later performance. Denenberg notes, for example, that one can find statements to the effect that the Bayley Developmental Test scores are not related to later IQ scores; or that experience in Head Start is not related to later school achievement; or that experiences during the first three to six months of life are not related to subsequent cognitive or perceptual measures.

"It is apparent," says Denenberg, "that such conclusions can have great impact upon the research activities within the developmental sciences, as well as influence social and political actions nationally. Thus it is quite important to examine the underlying logic concerning these conclusions to see whether they are justifiable." Denenberg believes that it is virtually impossible to make any meaningful statement concerning developmental relations in humans based upon the lack of significant correlations between early variables and later variables unless a test for interactional effects has been made.

Indeed, Denenberg argues that a linear causal (or correlational) approach is for the most part inadequate to describe developmental data. Instead, he advocates the framework offered by general systems theory, a field that developed because the two central concepts that had been used to explain the phenomena of science—linear causality and random probability—were considered inadequate to account for the innumerable interactions that are specific to living things and life processes. Abandoning the mechanistic approach of experimental science, general systems theory aims at a deeper understanding of the properties and principles of organized "wholes". Such an understanding can be attained only by studying a system as a complete entity, rather than by analyzing and "adding together" its component parts.

Denenberg views general systems theory as a compelling method for focusing intensively on individual subjects and their immediate environments. This is in marked contrast to both the correlational and experimental approaches, which measure each individual on the same variable and use group average statistics for purposes of both discovering general laws and characterizing the individual in a statistical or actuarial sense. If one is interested in gaining a deeper understanding of people as individuals, there are some obvious limitations to using group average statistics.

One problem, for example, is the requirement that all subjects be measured on the same variable. Denenberg points out that while this is necessary for statistical comparisons among individuals or groups, being limited to studying only those variables that are common to everyone yields an extraordinarily narrow view of the individual. And, he observes, "we do have a better understanding of a child when we know that person's sex, socioeconomic status, growth rate, IQ, school achievement scores, aptitudes, interests, etc. However, these kinds of measures tell us nothing about the child's style of communication, his or her play behavior, food preferences, the nature of interactions with parents, and the many other behavioral characteristics which we must know to describe the child as an 'interesting' human being (in contrast to describing the child as a 'statistical' human being)."

A further limitation of this approach to behavioral development has to do with the difficulty of analyzing group data according to general systems theory. Denenberg sees the developing infant together with its caregivers as a dynamic system—and he feels that the only way to really understand the laws that govern such systems is to study each individual system separately, instead of trying to work backwards from group averages.

For Denenberg, the advantage of studying single subjects is that one can gain a quicker and deeper appreciation of the individual *per se*, as in a clinical case history, where the objective is to portray an individual in as much depth and roundness as possible. Such an approach is generally considered "unscientific", since the clinician does not seek general laws. As Denenberg points out, however, clinicians and others have in fact extracted general principles from detailed studies of single subjects, and have successfully tested these principles on other individuals, Sigmund Freud being perhaps the most outstanding example.

Regardless of one's theoretical position, however, there are major obstacles to be overcome in working with single subjects. For one thing, it's difficult to separate, within a single individual, that individual's unique behavior patterns from features shared in common with others. Meaningful generalizations can be attained only from commonality, not from uniqueness. Once the obstacle of uniqueness is overcome, there remains the problem of determining just how general are one's generalizations.

General systems theory, to Denenberg, provides a way to reconcile the seemingly unscientific insights available only in intensive case studies with the requirements for rigor and replicability demanded of behavioral science. He outlines an approach to gathering information about single subjects and a method of testing for generality. In essence, Denenberg advocates treating each subject as a separate experiment. If there is an extensive enough data base, he says, it is possible to perform certain key statistical tests on a single individual and to obtain parameters that characterize that person. Then, if those parameters can be replicated in other subjects, one can assume that the phenomenon is generalizable beyond a single person.

For example, one researcher reported the following analysis of six infants: If the infant cried and was picked up within less than ninety seconds, the crying stopped very quickly. However, if the baby were allowed to cry for more than ninety seconds, it took a long time for the crying to subside. This ninety-second value was found in five of the six infants.

Another researcher studied a mother-infant pair in which the baby cried a great deal during its second week of life. Over the subsequent three weeks, the crying lessened. Analysis of the data revealed that at first the mother did not pick the infant up in less than ninety seconds, but she learned to do so over the ensuing weeks. Denenberg speculates that the reduction in crying was a function of the change in the mother's behavior over time, and suggests that if this same "learning curve" were found in other mother-infant pairs it might be a useful taxonomic category.

Denenberg stresses the importance of keeping separate the tactics used in conducting research in behavioral development and the perspectives that researchers have about their research. "Many years ago," he observes, "physicists gave up the belief that the universe could be described or explained in simple mechanistic terms, and they were compelled to turn to more complex models to account for their findings.

"I believe that we have also advanced in our study of behavioral development to a point where the basic assumption of mechanistic causality no longer offers us a perspective of sufficient breadth and depth to integrate the many findings we have obtained." Denenberg is convinced that general systems theory offers a far better perspective for viewing developmental phenomena, and that a powerful tactic involves the intensive study of individual units (including single subjects, the infant-caregiver pair, and the family constellation) in a naturalistic setting over some portion of the developmental time span. "To use this tactic efficiently," says Denenberg, "it is necessary to sample a wide range of behaviors in a sufficiently quantitative manner to allow for extensive statistical analyses *within* the individual unit. I am fully confident that the application of the concepts of general systems theory to such data will widen and change our perspectives and will suggest other

research directions for us to follow;
and that such an approach will aid in
giving us a richer and fuller
understanding of behavioral
development."

Evelyn B. Thoman, Ph.D.

Individuality in the Interaction Process

The dynamics of the early parent-infant relationship are a source of continuing fascination for behavioral scientists. A growing number of researchers, however, have grown dissatisfied with a one-dimensional model that focuses *only* on the baby or *only* on the parent. Their dissatisfaction has arisen from the difficulty of isolating specific caretaking practices that can be said to have an identifiable effect on the infant's development. Similarly, studies of infant behavior have failed to produce clear evidence that certain characteristics of the child will have a predictable impact on the parent.

Psychologist Evelyn B. Thoman of the Department of Biobehavioral Science at the University of Connecticut is among those who have relinquished a one-way view of parent-infant development in favor of acknowledging all the attendant complexities of a relationship in which a growing, changing, modifiable young being is cared for by an adult who, though apparently fully formed, is also subject to change by the relationship. Thoman and her colleagues are convinced that much more fruitful and reliable information can be gleaned from studying parents and infants within an interactional framework that emphasizes ongoing

reciprocity in the relationship.

In part, their model takes its inspiration from general systems theory, which provides a perspective that can better take parent-infant reciprocity into account. A major implication of systems theory, of course, is that one can no longer focus on single main effects or causal factors, but must be concerned with the interplay of numerous interacting forces. As Thoman says, "nonlinear relations are of the essence; nonstatic models are required." Thus, from an interactional point of view, it becomes difficult to conceive of either partner as "causing" the behavior of the other. For example, if a baby cries and is picked up by the mother, it is easy to conclude that the baby's cry caused the mother's behavior. On the other hand, if the mother picks up a sleeping infant, such an interpretation becomes obviously erroneous. In any case, as Thoman points out, "the immediately preceding behavior of either member of the pair often has only a trivial causal relationship to the subsequent behavior of the other member. Interaction is a process with an accumulation of its own history."

Since interaction is a process which involves change over time, Thoman advocates longitudinal studies of mothers and infants, and the careful collection of observational data that can help to identify and describe the nature of their ongoing patterns of interaction. The conceptual foundation of such research includes the following three premises: the notion that the mother-infant pair functions as a system; the assumption that a functioning system to be adequately understood, must be studied over time; and the assumption that the interactive process is expressed uniquely in each mother-infant pair. In practical terms this means that individual mother-infant pairs are studied intensively, with the researchers then abstracting from the observed behaviors some commonalities in individual mother-baby patterns that might reflect the essential nature of the interactive process.

This approach, it should be noted, is a marked departure from the study of groups of mother-infant subjects using group means as the source of generalizations. Obviously, the mean of a group reveals very little about the characteristics of any individual member. On the other hand, rigorous study of individual subjects has been considered well-nigh impossible without resorting to the old "case-study" approach, with its subjective interpretations and its notable lack of solid empirical data. Thoman points out that newer methodologies and techniques permit the collection of empirical data by recording precise behaviors with much less interpretive loading. She emphasizes that process questions are by nature very different from the judgmental interpretations so characteristic of clinical case histories.

At the same time, Thoman has found very useful some of the time-honored concepts handed down by sensitive clinicians, such as snychrony, mutual adaptation, and mutuality, which are really "systems" or "process" terms. According to Thoman, these can be defined empirically in terms of the rhythms or timing of mother or infant behaviors; or they can be defined in terms of specific behaviors on the part of either infant or mother—such as the infant's crying or the mother's caressing, where these behaviors are considered part of an ongoing sequence of interdependent behaviors.

As an example of asynchrony during the first month, Thoman describes one mother-infant relationship in which the infant, during active sleep, had a great deal of open-eyed REM (rapid-eye movement). The mother made it apparent that she mistook this activity for wakefulness, and, because she typically responded almost immediately to many of her infant's behaviors, she frequently picked the baby up for feeding when he was in fact asleep. Predictably, the feedings tended to go poorly, leading to many brief feeding episodes. Feeding became a difficult time for both mother and baby. Thoman notes that for another mother-infant pair the amount of open-eyed REM on the part of the baby might have very different relevance for their interactions. That is, synchrony or asynchrony in another relationship might involve quite different behaviors. "To understand the interactive process in any individual mother-infant pair," says Thoman, their behaviors must be observed intensively and the data analyzed to depict their individuality. Clues to generalizations regarding the nature of the interactive process will derive first from an understanding of the individuality expressed in many single mother-infant pairs, and secondly from identifying commonalities in the roles of specific behavior patterns for effecting mutuality in the relationship." For Thoman, the ultimate goal of research in this area is to gain a sufficiently keen understanding of the interactive process and its impact on infant development that accurate assessments (and short-term predictions) of individual mother-infant pairs will be possible.

The research just completed by Thoman and her colleagues is a fascinating naturalistic study of twenty mother-infant pairs over the first year of the babies' lives. All were first babies—thirteen boys and seven girls—whose mothers were enrolled in the study between their sixth and ninth months of pregnancy. A major objective was to identify the earliest individual patterns of infants and mothers in interaction, and to relate these early behavior patterns to those observed at one year of age.

Observations of mother and baby were made twice in the hospital; at home when the infants were two, three, four, and five weeks old; and then once again around the time of their first birthdays. Each of the early home observations was made during a continuous seven-hour period, with the observer carefully avoiding interaction with anyone in the household. Specific pre-coded behaviors were recorded every ten seconds throughout this period. They included the proximity of mother and infant to each other; the infant's position in space (i.e. whether he was being held, carried, etc.); mother-infant activity, such as feeding,

changing, bathing, or noncaretaking. Mother behaviors during these activities included talking to the baby, rocking, smiling, etc.; and infant behaviors included sucking, vocalizing, smiling, or moving about. The infant's behavioral state—quiet or active sleep, being alert, fussing, crying, etc.—was also noted. With the aid of a small electronic timing device, the presence or absence of some seventy-eight behaviors was recorded at ten-second intervals. When the babies were a year old, some of the earlier recorded behaviors were still appropriate, while others were added to include the babies' developing motor skills and verbal abilities.

From these lists of recorded behaviors, the researchers grouped together meaningful combinations of mother and/or baby behaviors. Some of these represented concurrent behaviors of the pair; for example, the baby might fuss or cry while being held by the mother; the mother might look at the baby during a period of fussing or crying; the baby might be in an alert state while being held; or mother and baby might be engaged in eye-to-eye contact. Other behaviors described only one member of the pair. These included characteristics of the infant's sleep states, the mother's stimulation of the baby, or the amount of time she spent near her baby. Thoman emphasizes that *all behaviors*—whether concurrent or involving only one member of the pair—were considered to be interactive. That is, they expressed, in one way or another, the nature of the mother-infant system.

While the total group of twenty infants and their mothers provided an important comparative function, of particular concern to Thoman and her colleagues were the patterns of individual babies. Thus, they selected two babies to compare and contrast with each other and with the total group. One mother-infant pair was of special interest because the baby, during the first five weeks of life, beginning with the earliest mother-infant contacts after birth, showed a most unusual response to being held or carried. When the mother picked her baby up, he typically became dazed, drowsy or fretful. In contrast, when left alone in his crib, the baby showed considerable alertness and spent time scanning his environment. At various times, the parents expressed their concern over the baby's "not liking to be held." Early observations indicated a dramatic difference between this mother-infant relationship and the others in the group in terms of the baby's varying degrees of alertness and irritability when being held or allowed to remain undisturbed in the crib. From these specific early indications, says Thoman, "one might have identified this as a 'relationship at risk' ".

Analysis of the data from the initial observations, says Thoman, confirmed the impression of early difficulty. During the first five weeks, this baby fussed more than the average for other babies in the group, and was especially irritable when being touched or held. Thoman reports, however, that the mother interacted with the baby a great deal—not just when performing caretaking activities, and she engaged in a lot of affectionate stimulation, such as patting and caressing. When the baby fussed or cried, the mother was highly likely to respond by stimulating or talking to him.

Thus, despite the baby's evident aversion to usual physical stimulation, Thoman and her colleagues described the mother's interaction with her baby as sensitive, and they predicted that the relationship would develop quite adequately.

Data from the one year observations fully confirmed the optimistic prediction made for this mother-infant pair. Thoman reports that at one year of age, this baby cried less than any other baby in the group during the home observations. She points out, incidentally, that the father was at home during these one-year observations, increasing the total interaction time to a level well above that of the group as a whole. According to Thoman, the mother's direct interactions with her baby were about the same as other mothers; however, they clearly reflected an adaptation to the infant's early aversion to body contact: This mother and baby had, overall, less physical contact than other mother-infant pairs, and what little there was occurred primarily at the initiative of the baby. Indeed, when there was physical contact, it tended to be baby's-body-to-mother's-legs rather than direct body-to-body contact. Thoman sees the extremely low level of physical contact between mother and baby as one indication of their mutual adaptation, and she describes the pair as showing an uncommonly high level of mutual responsiveness in a relationship that continued to be facilitative of the baby's development.

Thoman takes pains to explain that, as might be expected in any pair, there was not for this mother and baby a consistency in specific behaviors from the early weeks to one year, but rather an observable continuity in the way they related to each other. The positive development of this relationship is all the more striking when compared with another mother-infant pair who showed continuity of a different sort: the baby was visually unresponsive to the mother and the mother was relatively inattentive to the baby during the early weeks. At one year, there was still a mismatch in the timing of their attentiveness to each other; and their asynchrony was reflected in the baby's fretting and crying a great deal, although this baby had not been particularly irritable during the early weeks of life. Again, the patterning of interaction rather than specific behavior tells the story.

Thoman's research required a great deal of time and the collection of a vast amount of observational data on twenty babies in order to provide an empirical base for describing the complex nature of a single relationship. "By intensive, longitudinal study of an increasing number of individual mother-infant pairs," says Thoman, "we hope to find commonalities in patterns that will give clues to the nature of the processes involved in the development of the social responsiveness of mother and baby."

Louis W. Sander, M.D.

Changes in Infant and Caregiver Variables Over the First Two Months of Life: Regulation and Adaptation in the Organization of the Infant-Caregiver System

Psychiatrist Louis W. Sander of the University of Colorado Medical Center has long studied the influence of early parent-infant interaction on personality organization. Sander stands apart from most of the other researchers represented in this volume, however, because the questions guiding his research arose directly from clinical problems. His perspective is that of clinical psychiatry, rather than animal behaviorism or experimental psychology. This perspective provides a unique entree to a "systems" point of view. As Sander explains, "the psychiatric patient is a person whose coherence or integrity is threatened in his situation of adaptation. He sits before the therapist as a patient whose personality organization is to be changed.... The idea of psychotherapy seems to be for the therapist to sit with him and to interact, with the understanding that the organization of the patient's personality will change through an interactive process." Sander says that when he began in psychiatry, although he appreciated various aspects of personal interaction, he wanted to look closely and systematically at the beginnings of life "to search for a model of change in organization via some interactive process."

In the earliest days of life, as every parent is keenly aware, the initial task of adaptation for the new baby and the family is that of living together twenty-four hours a day, adjusting sleeping and waking times to day and night. A related problem in adaptation involves the continuing adjustments necessary between infant and caregiver. These adaptive interactions help to establish the basic regulation of the baby's sleeping, feeding, crying, and eliminating.

From such general observations, Sander's research questions gradually gained focus: How does adaptation to a pattern of sleeping-waking-eating, etc. over a twenty-four-hour period relate to the moment-by-moment adaptations in the interactions between infant and caregiver? In what way does adaptation at these two levels relate to the infant's sensory-motor functions?

Sander and his colleagues sought a conceptual understanding by considering temporal patterns in the life of the infant. They came to view the experience of birth as a profound disturbance in the temporal organization of fetal life. With birth, the familiar rhythms of maternal cycles are suddenly lost. At the same time, the newborn is exposed to new rhythmic inputs from both his own physiological sources and from new outer sources as well. It is clear, says Sander, that "the pre-empting task for the caregiver over the first three to four weeks of life is that of...restoring the temporal organization of the infant within its system of life support."

The problem, for Sander and his colleagues, was to figure out how "temporal organization" could be visualized in an infant-caregiver system, and then to devise a way to investigate it. A combination of two methodological approaches provided the answer: namely, continuous twenty-four-hour bassinet monitoring of infant states, and a strategy of event-recording of sequential interactions between infant and caregiver. "If we could *combine* data of 24-hour patterns of sleep and wakefulness with data of the adaptive employment of specific sensory-motor functions," Sander wondered, "would we find that disturbances in the one domain affected the developmental course taken in the other? If this were the case, how might the changing organization of the developing system be conceptualized to account for such an effect?"

Sander's current research is an ingeniously devised project aimed at describing changes in the organization of infant-caregiver interactions over the first two months of life. He and his colleagues studied twenty-seven infants divided into three time periods: Period I, the first ten days of life; Period II, days 11–29; and Period III, days 30–59. The three groups of infants, labeled A, B, and C, represented three differently constituted infant-environment systems.

Group C babies were with their natural mothers. Group A and B babies were not. During the first ten days, Group A babies were in a neonatal nursery, whereas Group B babies went to surrogate mothers almost immediately after delivery. (After ten days, babies in Groups A and B received the same kind of care.) Data collection was carried out by the two principal methods outlined above. Bassinet monitoring around the clock, day after day, provided the temporal framework of twenty-four-hour cyclic patterns of infant activity, quiescence, and crying and caregiver intervention. Sequential interaction between infant and caregiver was observed and recorded during feedings.

Of particular interest to Sander and his colleagues were changes in the infants' visual behavior over the two months. Infants were observed under both natural and experimental conditions.

Under the experimental condition, the infant was systematically shown a set of visual stimuli while lying in his familiar crib in a state of optimal quiet alertness. An observer recorded the occurrence of a number of precoded infant behaviors, such as looking at the stimulus, looking away, fussing, closing the eyes, etc. Three visual stimuli were used: a black and white line drawing of a face, the face of the experimenter (male), and the face of the caregiver (female). The faces of experimenter and caregiver were presented in a fixed sequence: still, nod, and social.

Confrontation with the human face, Sander and his colleagues found, provides a highly exciting stimulus for the awake, alert infant—a level of excitation that the infant must then regulate. His behavior may be that of avoiding, i.e., going from looking at the stimulus to peripheral looking or looking away, closing the eyes, or turning the head. The researchers noticed that with persistent confrontation, the baby's behavior might reflect increasing excitation, with flailing of arms and legs, or twisting of body and head, and finally perhaps culminating in fussing or crying. They found that a 60-second stimulus presentation could be regarded as a "test of limits." Sander notes that even after the first 30 seconds, many of the infants became uncomfortable or distressed, especially with the face under the "still" condition. The "nod" condition was somewhat less disturbing, and the black and white line drawing was almost invariably quieting.

The results showed a predictable increase in looking time from week two through week eight for all stimuli and all infants combined. Breaking down the looking time according to stimulus, the researchers found that the line drawing of the face was as high at week two as it would get within two months. In other words, the entire increase in looking time was in the babies' reactions to live faces. Furthermore, the still face failed to produce increased attention over the eight weeks, whereas the nodding and social faces did.

Although all three groups of infants began to react consistently to the stimuli by the sixth week, they took very different courses to get there. Group C got off to a slower start, and Group A babies were quite erratic, while Group B infants were the only ones who showed a significant discrimination between the male face and the caregiver's face, looking longer at the caregiver and actually seeming to avoid the

experimenter. "Group C infants," Sander reports, "appeared to be more specifically able and at an earlier point, to regulate visual impact by visual system behavior alone, i.e., looking away or closing their eyes."

In terms of time spent fussing and crying, there were highly significant differences among the three groups. Group A infants could not tolerate the stimuli as comfortably as could the other two groups, especially during the first month.

What, then, were the differences in the caregiving environments of these three groups? Although all infants were normal, and all were bottle fed, there were striking differences in their environments both pre and postnatally. The babies in Groups A and B were the firstborns of unwed mothers released for adoption. (The prenatal care these mothers received, however, was optimal, in that each of them lived in a well-run home for unwed mothers.) The babies in Group C were secondborns, cared for by their own mother over the two months of the project. The mothers were selected on the basis of a stable marriage, a previous normal and uneventful pregnancy, a normal firstborn with successful rearing to date, and an uncomplicated pregnancy with the study infant.

For the first ten days, caregiving differed for Groups A and B. Group A babies were kept in the hospital neonatal nursery until the morning of the eleventh day of life. They were given standard newborn care by multiple nurses, and were on a fixed, four-hour feeding schedule. In contrast, Group B infants went directly (12 to 24 hours after delivery) to a surrogate-mother nurse, who roomed in with the baby, around-the-clock, until the morning of day 11, each nurse on an individual basis with each infant, bottle feeding on an infant-demand schedule.

Period II began on the morning of the eleventh day and extended to day 29. Group A infants first began individual rooming in with surrogate-mother nurses on day 11, and Group B infants continued in their same rooming-in unit, but with a different surrogate-mother nurse than they had had during the first ten days. The surrogate mothers who participated in the project were middle-aged, registered private-duty nurses, each having successfully raised two children of her own, and having had experience in pediatric nursing and twenty-four-hour duty.

Thus, for Group A and B babies there were two changes of environment during the two months of the study: on day 11 and on day 29, when each A and B infant went to a different agency foster home until day 59. Agency foster mothers, most of whom had children of their own, were highly experienced caregivers, some having cared for as many as ten or 12 such foster infants in the past.

Sander reports that the newborn nursery experience over the first ten days for Group A babies was viewed by the research team as a most stressful time, largely because of the fixed feeding schedule. Between feedings, the infants might be allowed to cry for long periods unattended. Particularly during the first few days, says Sander, "bouts of crying were severe, continuing steadily for up to two hours or more until someone came, or until exhaustion supervened. After the seventh day, if the infant were unattended, the crying tended to be more intermittent and to come in

shorter bursts, with brief episodes of closed eyes and quietness between, from which the infant soon stirred and resumed crying."

Sander reports that the evidence derived from the continuous bassinet monitoring and from 24-hour observations of sleep and awake periods indicates that the stress endured by Group A babies during their first ten days of life reflected the marked delays between infant fussing and caregiver response. In addition to crying, this produced distress during feedings and an absence of any progress in day-night differentiation over the first ten days.

Group B babies, on the other hand, showed a very gradual achievement of day-night organization beginning well within the first ten days, and much less crying during this time. Each baby, moreover, showed a relatively stable pattern of crying, sleeping, and visual scanning. Group C differed from Group B in showing an early stability of napping periods, as well as day-night organization, so that the entire twenty-four hours began to possess a definite temporal structure.

Sander and his colleagues also examined the way infants of Groups A, B, and C used their eyes during feeding. Previous observations of natural mothers and their babies, says Sander, had impressed them with how intensely many infants gaze at their mother's face during a feeding. They also noticed that after the first few days of staring with such prolonged intensity, a number of the infants looked attentively at the mother's face only at the beginning of a feeding, and then appeared to need to gaze only occasionally or randomly back to the face for the remainder of the feeding. Sander suggests that such visual anchoring plays an important role in helping the infant regulate his behavior during feeding, particularly at stressful points.

The current project gained a heightened interest for Sander and his colleagues because of "an entirely unexpected dividend" that produced a second variable. By taking only one new infant at a time into the project, the researchers needed only two surrogate-mother nurses, and could assign each new infant in strict alternation to one nurse or the other without bias. Thus, half the Group A babies were cared for by Nurse X during Period II, and half were cared for by Nurse Y. For the Group B infants, those who had Nurse X during Period I had Nurse Y during Period II and vice versa. Afterwards, all A and B babies went to different foster mothers in Period III.

The two nurses had clear differences in caretaking styles, according to Sander. Nurse Y appeared to give the more specifically infant-oriented care. She was attentive to the infant's behavioral characteristics and insisted on giving priority to discovering individual differences and allowing each infant to guide her decisions about care. During feedings, she tended to cradle the infant in a way that enabled him to see her face. She also looked at the infant's face for cues to indicate his progress.

Nurse X, on the other hand, was much more oriented toward the researchers and regular hospital staff, and was good at making herself and everyone else comfortable. "At the same time," says Sander, "it appeared clear that she did not see the infants as separate individuals, and would say the same things about each baby."

She tended to hold the infants so that it was difficult for them to see her face, and wasn't particularly attentive to how an individual baby was managing a feeding.

Thus, the interest for Sander and his colleagues was not only in the differences among Groups Ax, Ay, Bx, By, and C and how they used their eyes during feedings, but also in the progressive development of each group over the two months of the study. Of particular interest is what happened in the second month of life to Group A and B babies, while they were each with different foster mothers whose variations in styles of feeding were fairly balanced for the two groups.

Averages of "infant regard" time (how much time the baby spent looking at the caregiver during feeding) were calculated for each infant. As in the experimental situation, in which visual stimuli were systematically presented, all three groups of babies arrived at a similar point by the end of the two months, but they followed different courses. Sander plotted the curves of the day-by-day changes in visual behavior for the babies of each group and for all groups of babies combined. The curve for all groups taken together shows that the peak of infant regard of caregiver is at the beginning of the second month of life, gradually diminishing thereafter.

An almost identical curve was shown by Group C babies alone. These, of course, were babies who were fed and cared for consistently by their own mothers over the two months of the project. According to Sander, the curve suggests that once the visual function achieves its full contribution to the regulation of the infant's state during feeding, its use becomes less and less essential, so that the infant's visual attention can be given to other things. In other words, the curve—for ABC together and for Group C alone—is viewed by Sander as "a trajectory over the two months representing the integration of the role of the visual system in the regulation of the feeding interaction."

The babies of Groups A and B showed different courses in integrating their visual resources. In stressful situations, these babies revealed different styles of visual behavior, and showed different vulnerabilities. For example, the transfer to a foster home appeared to be less distressing for group B babies as a whole than for Group A babies.

In that situation, under the stress of making a new adaptation to the foster home, Group B babies used their visual contact with the feeder *more* during feeding and Group A babies less. Here it is important to recall that during their first ten days of life in the nursery, Group A infants had no stability in the visual target of a caregiver's face, since the nurses changed with each shift and from day to day. In other words, visual cues were of least assistance to Group A infants in the initial feeding interaction, and were therefore presumably less useful later.

Sander outlines the trajectories shown by the babies in Groups Ax and Ay, Bx and By, which also varied predictably, showing different utilization of vision depending upon when in their earlier experience the need to become visually anchored to the feeder's face was being facilitated.

Having proposed a connection between "infant regard" of the feeder and the regulation of the feeding interaction, Sander was particularly interested in noting "distress events". These were defined as infant grimacing, turning away from or spitting out the nipple, gagging, spitting up, fussing, and crying.

Notably, the data showed that Bx infants, who demonstrated greater "infant regard" time in Period III (after spending days eleven to twenty-eight with Nurse X, who did not facilitate visual activity during feeding) were also having the highest distress scores in Period III. These were the infants who showed the least distress during the first ten days with Nurse Y. Sander suggests that vision may have come to play a relatively greater role in the earliest feeding regulation for these infants. Then, after a time of relative interference with visual contact during days 11 to 29, while being fed by Nurse X, distress events became prominent in Period III. Sander speculates that the infant's attempt to regain visual contribution to feeding regulation was confounded by the necessity to adapt to a new visual environment. He further proposes that "the initially greater role of visual function in regulating feeding in these infants set the stage for additional vulnerability at this later point in the trajectory of integration."

While Sander's work is far from conclusive, it offers some intriguing new hypotheses and suggests several new strategies of investigation. And while judgments about "good" or "bad" can obviously not be made within the confines of a two-month study, it does appear that there are different resources for, and vulnerabilities in, the regulatory mechanisms of the three groups that Sander studied under different conditions of adaptation. For Sander, "the importance of understanding mechanisms of regulation, and of connections between infant-caregiver interaction and the integration of infant function, is something necessitated now by the challenge of early intervention." The current interest in improving the development of infants at risk is enhanced by Sander's work.

Daniel N. Stern, M.D.

Rhythms of Maternal Behavior During Play

While increasing numbers of scientists are bent on unraveling the mysteries of the human infant's responsiveness to sounds, sights, movements, and tactile experiences, a few researchers have lately become interested in another dimension: the temporal patterning of sensory stimuli. Since all social stimuli are presented in time, an integral part of a baby's experience is his perception of how events are distributed, and how they change over time.

Dr. Daniel N. Stern of Cornell University, in collaboration with John Gibbon of Columbia University, has recently devoted particular attention to the role of timing in infant social responsivity. The timing element, says Stern, is as important "for watching a human face, which is almost always in motion, as it is for hearing vocalizations or experiencing bounces or tickles." Accordingly, his research attempts to answer the questions of how infants might estimate time intervals, form temporal expectancies and evaluate variations from the expected.

Stern points to several compelling reasons for focusing on the timing and temporal patterning of social behaviors and the infant's responses to them. He notes that during the earliest months of life, the interactive social system between mother and infant is a nonverbal one, important for its sensory properties, including its temporal properties, rather than for its associative or symbolic meaning. Moreover, it has been recognized that infants' social responses are closely tied to how incoming stimuli are distributed over time. For example, it has been shown that infants' smiles are best elicited when there is a rapid, accelerating increase in tension, followed by an abrupt drop in tension. Stern notes that the way a mother moves her face or body and the way she speaks to an infant are quite different from the way she typically interacts with another adult. Essentially, the mother tends to exaggerate her behavior when interacting with a baby, usually (though not always) by slowing down the tempo and rhythm of her movements, vocalizations, facial expressions, etc. These temporal exaggerations are often necessary to maintain the infant's interest and attention.

Further, there is increasing evidence to suggest the importance, early in infancy, of the formation of expectancies based on immediately preceding experience. While most such studies have examined visual and auditory stimuli, Stern argues that the temporal dimension of social behaviors is an essential part of mother-infant interactions, and that it therefore deserves special consideration.

In his examination of how infants form temporal expectancies, Stern focused on how mothers naturally behave with their infants. He concedes that to concentrate on the mother alone may render an incomplete picture; nonetheless, he has done so in the belief that "mothers are the most exquisitely tuned 'instruments' which nature has evolved and we 'possess' for assessing infant social capabilities. The study of naturally occurring infant-elicited maternal behaviors is quite likely to tell us much about what the infant either already 'knows' or is in the process of getting to know about human social behavior, and in particular, about the timing of human social behaviors."

To examine how an infant "clocks" maternal social behavior and estimates time intervals, three mother-infant pairs were studied under natural conditions in their homes. The infants were all healthy, firstborn females. Television tapes of naturally occurring play periods were taken at least once a week between the infants' third and fourth months of life. The mothers' only instructions were to behave normally.

As Stern suggests, a playful social interaction between mother and infant is hardly a smooth-running affair that unfolds with great regularity. Instead, there are bursts of activity and engagement ("time ins"), interspersed with periods of relative quiet ("time outs"). In order to establish criteria for what constitutes a recognizable burst and its boundaries, the television tapes were replayed and a magnetic tape event recorder was activated during each continuous maternal utterance and released during each silence. A computer analysis of the magnetic tape then yielded both a running record and the frequency distribution of the utterances and pauses. On the basis of this data, a three-second or longer pause was designated as a "time out" and anything in between pauses of this duration as "time in" episodes.

The choice of three seconds is supported by two different kinds of evidence. First, according to Stern, the average adult perceives a three-second pause as a lengthy break in the continuity of a stream of speech. The average vocal pause in adult dialogue is only 0.60 seconds, and the average speaker switching pause is only 0.64 seconds. Secondly, it has been established that delays of reinforcement greater than three seconds can significantly interfere with the contingent learning of human infants.

That is, if you don't present a reinforcement for an infant within three seconds, learning goes down rapidly, which suggests that that is the limit of whatever short-term memory is involved in contingent learning. Furthermore, Stern has observed that if the mother stops for three seconds, when she will resume becomes extremely and unlawfully variable because she may have stopped for one of a hundred reasons—because she has nothing more to say, or because she's fixing a bottle, or answering the telephone, or because someone else has walked into the room. Accordingly, Stern suggests that three seconds "may represent the point of an upward shift out of a predictable range, where the baby says, 'The devil with this, I'm going to stop counting till I get something a little more lawful coming in.'"

Stern and his colleagues were primarily interested in examining the infant's ability to track the timing of sequences of maternal behaviors as they occur within "time in" periods. Therefore, they selected sections of the television tapes which included "time in" episodes consisting of at least eight separate utterances (continuous vocalizations of one or more words). Each utterance and its successive pause made up an "onset-to-onset interval". The mother's nonverbal phrases, head movements, and facial displays were analyzed and scored in the same manner. The resulting data consisted of the duration of onset-to-onset intervals 1) of successive utterances in which the same verbal content was repeated; 2) of successive utterances which were not repetitious; and 3) of nonverbal repetitious movements that make up the games that mothers play with their babies.

Timing can play a communicative role in social behavior only if infants can estimate time intervals, develop expectancies of when an anticipated behavior ought to happen, and evaluate deviations from the expected. Stern first sought to determine what innate capabilities the infant might possess to keep track of time. The researchers observed that at the beginning of a "time in" period, the infant listens intently to the first few of his mother's utterances and the pauses between them. Presumably, if the onset-to-onset time of utterances is fairly regular, the infant develops an accurate expectation for the tempo of the "time in" period which could be regarded as an estimate for the time of the next vocal production.

Assuming that a central tendency of the infant's mental life involves the creation of expectancies and the evaluation of discrepancies from the unexpected, the ideal temporal stimulus could not be absolutely regular and fixed. If it were, there would be no deviations to evaluate and nothing to continue to engage the infant's mental process. On the other hand, if deviations around the expected were too large or irregular, the infant would presumably be incapable of perceiving them as deviations, since they would be unrelated to the expected referent. From what we know of the infant's attentional and cognitive processes, says Stern, it follows that "a temporal stimulus best suited to maintain interest and engagement would have a generally regular tempo (to allow for the formation of expectancy) but with a limited, or at least lawful, variability (to engage and maintain his evaluative processes)."

Stern and his colleagues found that during "time in" episodes, the mother generally establishes a fairly regular tempo for her behavior. This tempo may change suddenly at any point, but generally does so only after a period of "time out", consisting of a shift in the nature of her engagement or strategy with the infant. The problem that then faces the infant is one of "figuring out" the new timing, in which both tempo and variability may be considerably altered. Stern suggests that the mother can switch to any tempo she wants and the infant will automatically readjust his expectancies. This he calls a "scalar unit timer". In other words, according to Stern, the mother is able to maintain a reasonably consistent and high level of infant interest because the "scalar timing" of her utterances matches the timing process employed by the infant to evaluate temporal stimuli. She is, in short, able to provide the "ideal" temporal stimulus, one that has a degree of regularity in conjunction with lawful variability.

Suppose, however, that the mother wished to heighten the infant's attention rather than simply to maintain it, or to attract it if it were not directed toward her. One of the more striking features of maternal social behavior is the extraordinary amount of repetition—in speech, head and body movements, facial expressions. Stern found that whether he was scoring verbal or nonverbal behavior, as much as 40 percent of all vocal phrases and movement "phrases" such as head nod, were repeats of the immediately preceding behavior. The frequent use of repetion in the early months, Stern suggests, can have the quality of a "now hear this" signal.

When the duration of a pause exceeds some expected level, a "time out" period starts and the infant resets his unit timer for the next tempo value. But when the variance is too low, that is, when a repititious run occurs, the timing structure is altered and the infant's attention is focused on the repeated content itself, with an accompanying heightening of arousal and intensity in the communication system.

Stern and his colleagues determined the attention-getting effect of repetition by comparing all the times the infant turned to gaze at the mother during a repetitive run with all the times the infant turned to gaze at the mother when these conditions were not met. They found that visual attention-getting was significantly greater during repetitions.

After the infant's attention has been refocused by repetition, however, he quickly becomes accustomed to it; to maintain his interest, a new and different repetitive run is required. According to Stern, the mother appears to use the timing characteristics of the early part of the repeating sequence to refocus the infant's attention. Having done that, she can then reintroduce greater and greater amounts of variability betweeen successsive units for one of two ends. By the time a sequence of four or five repeated units is finished, the amount of variability that has been reintroduced begins to approach that seen in "normal", nonrepetitive utterances. The infant has been, so to speak, eased back into a position where his scalar unit timer will again begin to process the normal flow of maternal speech—but at a higher level of attentiveness. In a sense, says Stern, "the mother breaks up the temporal structure of her stimulation and then progressively reconstitues it so as to bring the infant along with her at a different level."

Secondly, as the repetitive run gets longer and more variable, it takes on unusual properties, becoming in a sense the inverse of music, where the beat remains the same but the words or melody keep changing. Stern suggests that these short sequences of behavior with their rather striking features may be used by the mother to alter not only the baby's attentional processes, but also his level of arousal and affective responses.

Finally, Stern and his colleagues analyzed the facial, gestural, and positional movements made by mothers as they played with their infants. They found that, as for vocalizations, the temporal organization of these behaviors conformed to a scalar process. Moreover, the timing of repetitive movements, such as those constituting simple games like "peek-a-boo", was highly similar to that of repeating vocal sequences. This suggests that temporal structures across all sensory modalities may serve the same communicative functions.

The work of Stern and his colleagues clearly points up the potentially significant role that time may play in the infant's responsiveness to his social environment. Of particular interest is the intimate link between affect and timing. A common example of the influence of timing on affective state is in the use of the lullaby, which, as Stern observes, not only has a characteristic tempo, but as actually used, one of its important features is to introduce a temporal change, the progessive slowing of tempo and decreasing of loudness at just the right point. Similarly, Stern notes that when a baby is upset and crying, "the mother will frequently speed up the tempo of her behavior to 'top' or override his, and then slowly and progessively decrease the tempo to bring the baby back down to a quieter state."

An interesting question in this regard is whether or not the level of affect associated with particular temporal distributions may differ depending on developmental age or personality tendencies. Stern also speculates that strong emotions could distort the operation of the scalar unit timer, thus "breaking up" the smooth flow of social behavioral responsiveness. Stern notes that this would be similar to Freud's first

theory of neurosis—that when something traumatic happens, it is received in an altered state of consciousness, so that it is in effect processed in the brain in a different temporal world, almost like a dream world. "The reason you can't integrate it and it stays neurotic is that it happened while you were in a different state of consciousness. Certainly experience has shown that there are a lot of events besides taking drugs that distort time."

Finally, it seems possible that these lines of inquiry may contribute to our understanding of abnormal infants. An inability to form temporal expectancies or to evaluate temporal intervals could, despite the intactness of other sensory and cognitive processes, cause a child to respond inappropriately (or to fail to respond) to social behaviors, and would also tent to disrupt general learning processes.

Before any of these possibilities can be investigated, however, Stern suggests that "our greatest need is to 'hear directly' from the infant concerning his capabilities of forming temporal expectancies." This will require finer behavioral analyses and the measurement of physiological indices. Only with such evidence can we go beyond description and speculation to a fuller understanding of "the infant's social responsiveness in the fourth dimension."

Discussant's Summary

In addition to the researchers whose work-in-progress was presented, several eminent people were invited by Johnson and Johnson to participate in the conference as discussants. Their generally insightful comments and critiques, summarized below, enlivened the conference proceedings and served a vital synthesizing function as well. In some cases, they also contributed important new information.

Arthur H. Parmelee

Arthur H. Parmelee, Professor of Pediatrics and head of the Division of Child Development at U.C.L.A., is a distinguished clinician who has sought to bring an interactional perspective to the area of risk assessment and prediction. So-called "risk scoring systems" were initially developed to determine risk for mortality or morbidity in the neonatal period. Parmelee has come to view most of them with considerable skepticism because, while very short-term predictions are possible, most neonatal risk items bear very little relationship to later behavior. In fact, Parmelee doesn't like to use the word "risk" at all, since as he points out, it is frequently unclear what the infants are at risk *for*.

"Social and environmental factors are so powerful," explains Parmelee, "that any biological risk item, even with associated deviant neonatal behavior, isn't very predictive of later behavior." Noting that babies are born with many selfrighting tendencies, Parmelee is hopeful that further research will yield a more detailed understanding of what the compensating mechanisms are. His co-worker, Dr. Bechwith, has found that babies who are sickest in the neonatal period often get the best "mothering scores" at one month. "What cues the mothers were reading that induced them to provide compensatory mothering we don't know," says Parmelee. "The difference in later performance seems to be whether or not these mothers and babies can sustain these positive interactions."

Parmelee observes that there are many behavioral contradictions to biological risk; he points out, for example, that in any obstetric risk scoring system, being a firstborn increases the risk. In the first two years, however, being a first and only child seems to be beneficial as far as behavioral assessments are concerned. Parmelee suggests that "there are probably many more such contradictions between perinatal biological risk for immediate mortality and morbidity and later behavioral and environmental compensatory processes."

With premature babies, who are at much greater risk at birth than full-term infants, it's often difficult to balance the advantages of continuous contact between mother and baby at home versus the disadvantages of caring for a very fragile and generally unresponsive baby. For Parmelee, the critical issue is support for the mother.

"With full-term babies," he explains, "the first three months of life are a struggle for survival for the parents, particularly the mother. The frequent feedings, disrupted sleep, and 24-hour care are a difficult burden. With the full-term infant, after about six to eight weeks life improves—crying lessens, sleep periods are longer, and the baby gives a rewarding smile so that by three months life is tolerable. The mother of the pre-term infant sent home four weeks before term has an extra month of this difficult struggle in addition to her concern about the baby's survival. The key issue is the organization of support services for the parents of pre-term infants. If you do provide that service, then there's much to be gained by having the mother and baby together this extra month. If you don't provide support service the mother can fall apart under this stress and you lose what you tried to gain."

Furthermore, Parmelee notes, the minute either the baby or the mother is sick, the potential for attachment is disrupted. For the pre-term infant, it's a given that the attachment problem is distorted; but, says Parmelee, "you can't assume that putting a very sick baby in the mother's arms is going to promote attachment." He believes that it is a much more complex process that probably extends over the whole first year or longer—which is what makes the provision of support services so important.

As a pediatrician, Parmelee is highly concerned that there be careful documentation of exactly what happens behaviorally in pre-term nurseries. He's concerned, he says, "that we're going ahead with interventions when we can't measure the outcomes. We've gone through the period of making babies blind because we thought oxygen was exceedingly good, crippling babies with jaundice because we thought a lot of Vitamin K was good. In other words, there have been many things that we've done, which were easily justified but were wrong. We need to document exactly what it is we're doing, why we're doing it, where we're starting from."

Harriet L. Rheingold

Harriet L. Rheingold, Research Professor of Psychology at the University of North Carolina, is among the most highly respected scientists in the field of early infancy. She is therefore in a unique position to survey methodological issues and to suggest further directions for reasearch.

Like Yarrow and Anderson, Rheingold is concerned about the "disorderly" data base from which inferences about the interactive process are drawn. Studies tend to vary so widely in setting, directions to parents, and behaviors recorded, she believes, that general statements of principles become virtually impossible. Rheingold is convinced that rigorous experimental designs are not only possible, but urgently necessary. Comparisons between behaviors in different settings can be made, for example, and the effect of different instructions to parents can be assessed. "For without knowledge about such elementary facts," says Rheingold, "firm statements of relationships cannot be built."

On the issue of settings, Rheingold is most articulate. She decries the current tendency to elevate the study of parent–child relations in the home because, to her, the choice of environment depends entirely upon the question or questions the investigator sets out to answer. "It cannot be held that only observations made in 'natural' environments are valid," says Rheingold. "What is a natural environment? What are the special advantages of studying infants and their parents where they spend all of their time, most of their time, or some of their time? As for laboratories, although they may conjure up images of Skinner boxes in the minds of some, they in fact may present quite ordinary and even homelike settings. The question to be asked . . . is 'more natural for what?' "

In terms of the generalizability of findings from laboratory to home or home to laboratory, Rheingold believes that any behavior observed in the laboratory must also occur outside. While she acknowledges that it is something of a feat to design laboratory studies or reproduce behavior that occurs elsewhere, she emphasizes that it is a feat that has often been accomplished. "There is no sound reason for thinking that behaviors in the laboratory are not normal, natural, representative, and generalizable. Infants and mothers do not have one set of behaviors for the laboratory and a totally different,

mutually exclusive set for outside the laboratory." Ideally, of course, according to Rheingold, researchers ought to be able to move freely between environments.

Rheingold is also concerned about the need for replications. She concedes that in the area of parent–child studies, where massive amounts of data are gathered, sometimes over relatively long periods of time, replications in the exact sense often seem prohibitive in terms of time and effort. Yet without replications, in Rheingold's view, the whole field suffers from the absence of a sound structure from which to draw conclusions or on which to build further studies.

In another vein, Rheingold is critical of the tendency, among her colleagues, to confer special status on the mother–infant relationship. "It is past time," she says, "to pay some attention to the fathers." She exempts as "too limited" studies of fathers' absence and of "contests" between fathers and mothers and unfamiliar persons in studies of attachment, and predicts that future studies will show that the father–infant relationship is not subsequently different from that of the mother and infant.

Rheingold also supports a more imaginative use of animal models in the study of early social behavior. She recommends choosing different species for different questions, making as precise a match as possible between the questions and the social organization and behavioral characteristics of the species. For example, if one were interested in the nature and extent of paternal care and its effect on the young, one would choose as an animal model a species in which the father stays with the mother and infant and participates in the infant's care.

Although Rheingold is a strong advocate of the intelligent use of models, she is not sanguine about the use of the computer as a model for the developing infant. "The use of the language of the computer," says Rheingold, "of terms like 'input', 'output,' 'preprogrammed,' and 'information processing,' while useful as shorthand, often seems to suggest that we know more than we really do. Labels do not explain. Their faddish use can persuade us that we have ended our search when in fact it has just begun."

Kathryn Barnard

Kathryn Barnard, Professor of Nursing at the University of Washington in Seattle, brings a clinical perspective to bear on the work of her more research oriented colleagues. Barnard is particularly interested in the infant states, and the modulation of behavioral arousal, such as depicted in the work of Sander. According to Barnard, the infant's own ability to come from non-aroused to aroused states, plus the caretaker's recognition of this process, will have a powerful influence on the quality of interaction and social responsiveness.

She offers a telling anecdote from her own work with premature babies, in which the mother and nurse were videotaped at separate times as they took the infant out of the incubator to feed. Barnard says she was particularly impressed, as the tapes were played back, with the differences between the two caretakers: "The mother went through a very elaborate

procedure of slowly unwrapping, touching, moving the baby's arms, stroking, jiggling, and bouncing the baby for about 20 minutes to bring the infant up to an aroused state, and then she began the feeding. When she was done feeding, she brought the infant down using non-arousal stimuli which were less intense and more regular." In contrast, when the nurse picked up the baby, she immediately began bottle feeding with no attempt to raise the infant's arousal level. Barnard notes that the premature infant is generally less responsive during the early months and so provides an interesting focus of study when considering the origins of social responsiveness.

Like Rheingold, Barnard is concerned about the father's involvement—or lack of it—with a new baby. After years of observation, Barnard has come to view the mother as a sort of "gatekeeper"; that is, how involved the father becomes depends a great deal on how much the mother will allow him to be. That in turn may depend on the infant's threshold for stimuli and novelty. Some infants can simply deal better than others can with variety and tempo changes.

She tells the story of one couple who went through prepared childbirth together. The father participated in the labor and delivery and was quite enthusiastic about parenting. At about six months postpartum, Barnard recalls, he said "this is a bunch of nonsense; it's no partnership." What was happening, Barnard explains, is that every time he would try to interact with the baby, she would begin to scream. Observations of the mother, on the other hand, revealed that she was using a unique and specific tempo in her interactions with the baby. She would approach the infant very slowly, and gradually increase the rhythm of her behavior, whereas the father's pattern was to approach the infant without a buildup. At about eight or nine months, the mother began to recognize this and could help her husband modulate his behavior, while she in turn began to vary her behavior with the infant more.

Barnard believes that some sex differences—such as the male voice and characteristic gestural differences—relate directly to this issue of arousal. "Some infants need a more modulated course to get to an 'interactive alert state.' High arousal techniques, larger, sharper movements, high voice variability, etc. may serve to bring infants to a high level of arousal too fast, resulting in an overload and subsequent irritability."

Barnard's work has led her to speculate that "if we really are to understand the origins of social responsiveness in the infant, we probably will need to go back in time looking for the answers which abound in the patterns of communication that the couple, the mother and father, have prenatally. Their ability to interact with each other will form the basic fabric for the character of the infant's emerging behavior. Therefore, if you look first at each partner's ability to signal and respond in an interaction, you will have a beginning constant to put into the prediction equation of how the infant will respond."

John H. Kennell

John H. Kennell, Professor of Pediatrics at Case Western Reserve University, is perhaps best known for his studies of mother–infant interaction in the period right after birth. He has shown that if a mother and her full-term baby are together in those first few moments or hours, there will be significant effects on the mother's behavior for months and years afterward, and that the babies will be different as well. In this regard, Kennell suggests, humans may not be so different from animals. For example, a mother goat becomes firmly attached to her kid within the first ten minutes of its life. But if for some reason the kid is removed during those early minutes, the mother goat will just as firmly reject it.

While human attachment—or rejection—is hardly so extreme because the human has remarkable, adaptive capacities, Kennell urges careful attention in clinical care and in infancy studies, to the details of mother-infant contact or separation in the first postpartum minutes and days. Many of the disturbances in the state and behavior of infants are due to lack of mother–infant contact in the first hours after birth, when both are in a maximally receptive, alert state. Kennell believes that our practice of starting babies out in the standard hospital nursery environment with multiple caretakers may make adjustment to care at home much more difficult.

Indeed, Kennell looks at many of our child care practices from an historical, evolutionary perspective. He explains that throughout most of human history people lived as hunters and gatherers. "In this phase of existence which is very recent in an evolutionary sense," says Kennell, "the mother carried the baby on her body all the time. The two slept together and because the mother usually had to walk great distances each day, she could only carry one baby. This had a powerful influence on birth control, with three to four years the minimal spacing."

Kennell further speculates that the large amount of infant crying in this country is in part a result of baby care practices that differ so markedly from the close contact, abundant body movement, and frequent nursing of our hunter–gatherer ancestors. "Have we in our studies," he asks, "paid too much attention to visual and auditory behavior, because we as adults are interested in vision and hearing, and neglected other modalities such as tactile and vestibular?"

Kennell points to some evidence from animal studies as being suggestive of how babies lived and were cared for in past centuries. Ben Schaul surveyed the composition of breast milk in more than 100 mammalian species and found that the milk differed greatly in protein and fat content. Interestingly enough, this bore no relation to the size of the animals. However, there was a strong correlation between milk composition and frequency of feeding, with a distinct difference in protein and fat concentration between infrequent feeders whose mothers spend long periods away, and continuous feeders who had ready access to the breast.

In certain rabbits, for example, feedings occur once every 24 hours. The mother's milk has a high caloric density and a high protein and fat content. In the great blue whale, feedings are also widely spaced and the milk has a similarly high concentration of protein and fat. In contrast, higher primates have constant access to the nipple, feed nearly continuously, and the milk has low protein and fat content. Human milk is almost identical to that of the other primates and has the characteristic protein and fat content of continuous feeders. According to Kennell, in developing countries observations of mothers sleeping with their infants throughout the night confirm this pattern. The largest interval between feedings was 20 minutes. And, significantly, there was virtually no crying in those cultures.

Furthermore, animals that are fed at widely spaced intervals show the fastest sucking rates. The rabbit empties the breast in four to five minutes, for example, while the stump-tailed Macaque monkey feeds for 10 to 30 minutes at 30-minute intervals. Kennell points out that the slow rate of human suckling "provides highly suggestive support for adaptations in the baby to match those in the mother for continuous contact between them." How did the change to four hour feeding schedules come about in the United States? Rigid feeding schedules, says Kennell, were strongly recommended by German pediatricians who dominated pediatric concepts at the turn of the century. In spite of what we recommend about demand feeding, the four-hour schedule is still an expectancy of a great proportion of mothers. We need to ask what is that doing to babies.

And , he continues, in regard to timing influences on the infant, "I wonder if the infant's timer isn't already set through the nine months of pregnancy and then readjusted in that early postnatal period, with the mother's speech to the baby, when mother and baby are together."

Bibliography

Ben Schaul, DM: Notes on hand-rearing various species of mammals, *International Zoo Year Book 4:* 300, 1962.

Bower, T. G. R., *Development in Infancy,* W. H. Freeman & Co., San Francisco, 1977.

-----, *The Perceptual World of the Child,* Harvard University Press/Open Books, 1977.

-----, *A Primer of Infant Development,* W. H. Freeman & Co., San Francisco, 1977.

Bruner, J., M. Cole, B. Lloyd (Eds.) (The Developing Child Series), *The First Relationship: Infant and Mother,* Cambridge, Harvard University Press, 1977, D. Stern.

Crook, C. K., Neonatal Sucking: Effects of quantity of the response-contingent fluid upon sucking rhythm and heart rate, *Journal of Experimental Child Psychology,* 1976, *21,* 539–548.

-----, and L. P. Lipsitt, Neonatal nutritive sucking: effects of taste stimulation upon sucking rhythm and heart rate, *Child Development,* 1976, *47,* 518–522.

Denenberg, V. H. and E. B. Thoman, From animal to infant research, In T. D. Tjossem (Ed.), *Intervention Strategies for High-Risk Infants and Young Children,* Baltimore: University Park Press, 1976.

Eisenberg, Rita B., Auditory competence in early life: *The Roots of Communicative Behavior,* University Park Press, Baltimore, Md., 21202 (1976).

Klaus, M., and J. Kennell: *Maternal-Infant Bonding,* St. Louis, Mosby Co., 1976.

Kobre, K. R., and L. P. Lipsitt, A negative contrast effect in newborns, *Journal of Experimental Child Psychology,* 1972, *14,* 81–91.

Korner, A. F., Early stimulation and maternal care as related to infant capabilities and individual differences, *Early Child Development and Care,* 1973, *2,* 307–327.

-----, and R. Grobstein, Visual alertness as related to soothing in neonates: Implications for maternal stimulation and early deprivation, *Child Development,* 1966, *37*(4), December, 867–876

-----, and E. B. Thoman, Relative efficacy of contact and vestibular stimulation on soothing neonates, *Child Development,* 1972, *43*(2), June, 443–453.

-----, -----, Visual alertness in neonates as evoked by maternal care, *Journal of Experimental Child Psychology,* 1970, *10,* August, 67–78.

-----, and H. C. Kraemer and M. E. Haffner and L. Cosper, Effects of waterbed flotation on premature infants: A pilot study, *Pediatrics, 56*(3), 1975, 361–367.

Lipsitt, L. P., The study of sensory and learning processes of the newborn, In J. Volpe (Ed.), *Clinics in Perinatology,* Vol. 4, No. 1, Philadelphia: W. B. Saunders, 1977, pp. 163–186.

-----, (Ed.), *Developmental Psychobiology: The Significance of Infancy,* Hillsdale, NJ, Lawrence Erlbaum Associates, Publishers (distributed by Wiley), 1976.

-----, Perinatal indicators and psychophysiological precursors of crib death, In F. D. Horowitz (Ed.), *Early Development Hazards: Predictors and Precautions,* American Association for the Advancement of Science, 1978, in press.

-----, The synchrony of respiration, heart rate, and sucking behavior in the newborn, In J. C. Sinclair and J. B. Warshaw (Eds.), *Biologic and Clinical Aspects of Brain Development,* Mead Johnson Symposium on Perinatal and Developmental Medicine, No 6, 1975, pp. 67–72.

-----, and M. G. Mustaine and B. Zeigler, Effects of experience on the behavior of the newborn, *Neuropadiatrie, 1977, 8,* pp. 107–133.

-----, and B. M. Reilly and M. J. Butcher and M. M. Greenwood, The stability and interrelationships of newborn sucking and heart rate, *Developmental Psychobiology, 1976, 9,* pp. 305–310.

Lozoff, B., and G. Brittenham and M. A. Trause and J. Kennell and M. Klaus, The Mother-Newborn Relationship—Limits of Adaptability, *Journal of Pediatrics, 91*(1): 1–12, 1977.

Schaffer, R. (Ed.), "The Infant's Stimulus 'World' During Social Interaction: A Study of the Structure, Timing and Effects of Caregiver Behaviors," In: *Interactions in Infancy,* The Loch Lomond Symposium, London: Academic Press, 1977, pp. 177–203.

Thoman, E. B., The role of the infant in early transfer of information, *Biological Psychiatry, 1975, 10,* pp. 161–169.

-----, Modification of responsiveness to maternal vocalization in the neonate, *Child Development, 1977, 48,* pp. 563–569.

-----, and P. T. Becker, Individual patterns of mother-infant interaction, In G. P. Sackett and C. C. Haywood (Eds.), *Application of Observational/Ethological Methods to the Study of Mental Retardation,* Baltimore: University Park Press, 1978.

-----, and M. E. Gaulin-Kremer, Correlates of human parental behavior: A review, In H. Musaph and J. Money (Eds.), *Textbook of Sexology,* 1977, ASP Biological and Medical Press BU, Amsterdam, The Netherlands, Elsevier/North-Holland.

-----, and A. F. Korner and H. C. Kraemer, Individual consistency in behavioral states in neonates, *Developmental Psychobiology, 1976, 9,* pp. 271–283.

Yarrow, L. J., Historical perspectives on infant development, In *Handbook of Infant Development,* Wiley-Interscience, In press.

-----, and F. A. Pedersen, The interplay between cognition and motivation in infancy, In M. Lewis (Ed.), *Origins of Intelligence:*

Infancy and Early Childhood, New York: Plenum Publishing Corp., 1976, pp. 376–399.

-----, and J. L. Rubenstein and F. A. Pedersen, *Infant and Environment: Early Cognitive and Motivational Development,* Washington, D.C.: Hermisphere Halsted-Wiley, 1975.

-----, and F. A. Pedersen and J. L. Rubenstein, Mother-infant interaction and development in infancy, In Leiderman, P. H. and Tulkin, S. (Eds.), *Cultural and Social Influences in Infancy and Early Childhood,* New York: Academic Press, 1977, pp. 539–564.

-----, and R. P. Klein and S. Lomonaco and G. A. Morgan, Cognitive and motivational development in early childhood, In Friedlander, B. Z., Sterritt, G. M. and Kirk, G. (Eds.), *The Exceptional Infant: Assessment and Intervention,* Vol. 3, New York, Bruner/Mazel, 1975.